Advent Women

Biblical Women –
A Force Before Their Time

by

PATRICIA BATSTONE

Front cover: *Knit and Natter Knitivity* © Mark Lilley, Wirksworth Library 2016

Back cover Nativity Tableau, Ashbourne Methodist Church 2017

Illustrations   © The Estate of James Byron-Archer

British Library Cataloguing in Publication Data.
A catalogue record for this book is available from the British Library

ISBN 978 0 86071 762 1

A Commissioned Publication Printed by
MOORLEYS
Print, Design & Publishing
info@moorleys.co.uk · www.moorleys.co.uk

CONTENTS

ADVENT WOMEN

is dedicated to the members of the Women's Fellowships who, during my fifty-four years as a Methodist Local Preacher ministering in the Warwick and Leamington Spa, Kineton, Hull Trinity and West, Gravesend and Dartford, Exeter, Tiverton, Sidmouth and Bridport, Exmouth and Budleigh Salterton and Derbyshire Dales Circuits, invited me to share these women's stories. Many of these groups have since closed, with congregations swallowed up in circuit reorganisations, but I remember them now with love and gratitude for their encouragement and inspiration.

WOMEN AT THE PASSION

Luke 23:26-31,44-24:10

They were there, Lord, as you suffered,
those who loved you -
mainly the women.
For three years they had hovered in the background,
serving, listening, devotedly caring;
now, when the men shy away,
they are there at the forefront,
longing to give you some small crumb of comfort,
determined to love you to the end,
though their hearts break.

They had their reasons -
some out of gratitude for health and freedom -
Mary of Magdala,
Susanna, wealthy widow,
Joanna, an upmarket woman of means,
even Peter's ageing mother-in-law;
Salome, the pushy mother, outstaging her sons,
and Mary,
your loving, broken mother, too -
all equal at the foot of your cross,
forgiven sinners, reconciling gift and given,
one in you, helplessly watching you die,
waiting to take down your bruised body
and tenderly wrap in fine new linen and lay you to rest,
anointing you with spices, mingled with tears.

No wonder it was to them that the first signs of
resurrection came -
only they had gone with you to death.
Only you could love them to life.

ADVENT WOMEN

INTRODUCTION

Of making many books there is no end ... declared The Preacher (also known as Quoholeth)[1] – and that is certainly true of books about Biblical characters, especially women. They have been fictionalised, treated in their historical and geographical contexts by academics in their field, presented as moral exemplars, taken literally or considered symbolically as archetypes or originals of their time – myths transmitted orally and then written down as 'historical facts', focus for meditations, or simply good stories whose subjects have been classified as heroines or villains, ordinary or extraordinary, demeaned or romanticised. Norah Lofts described them as 'psychological types'.[2] Several poets have attempted first-person presentations, but as I have mentioned elsewhere, there needs to be an authentic voice to each subject, but this is often eclipsed by the writer's own style.[3] Sometimes they are even looked at as real people, flesh and blood individuals with individual and independent lives, capable of thinking for themselves and doing magnanimous deeds either to please God or to challenge men.

But Quoholeth also said, *much study is a weariness to the flesh.* and that is a warning to keep it simple. So this book is not intended to be a definitive or academic study, rather to stimulate thought – hence the questioning approach that leaves readers to draw their own conclusions. Studies of a deeper, more academic nature will be found listed in the Bibliography.

Rather than present them as 'characters', as though they were players on a stage or film set, I like to think of them as real, living women – women in many ways being and behaving before their time – out of kilter with the world they were living in – often subjects in a patriarchal society – even beyond the Old Testament period – sometimes women with whom we may find ourselves identified.

Hence, I call them 'Advent Women' – women-in-waiting, waiting for their moment, perhaps in some instances a little too impatiently. At others they seem to have unexpectedly had their 'moment' thrust upon them. And Advent, for me, **is** waiting – but not just for Christmas!

1

Yet in reality much of Old Testament society, once established as a kingdom, lived in waiting – waiting for the promised Messiah who would deliver them from their evil, godless invaders. And when that first waiting period was fulfilled it was women who became some of his most ardent followers. And when they had seen him die and rise and go away again with an oblique promise of "I'll be back" – they became women in waiting all over again.

Only our New Testament women didn't stand still. Like their Old Testament predecessors they burst the bounds of convention and were unafraid to claim his allegiance and further his cause by any means possible. They were pioneers. They made and prepared the way for countless women to follow without even knowing what they were doing and how they would impact future generations. Advent brings new things – new life, new meaning, new direction into the world – and they did all these things. Advent Women indeed!

My particular interest in Biblical women arose out of what can only be described as 'an incident'. My husband had been to a Bible study group where the decision was reached that women shouldn't be preachers - and he was fairly newly married to one! That incident set me on an exploration into the lives of many Biblical women, the reading of countless books about them, and the giving of numerous talks at women's meetings, some of which material is used here. The results may beg many questions, some of them uncomfortable – and encourage the asking of many more.

Interestingly, when I had exhausted the 'usual suspects' I asked the secretary of each meeting to which I was invited to consult her meeting and ask who they would like to hear about. The result took me to some very unexpected places! One secretary asked me to speak about the Shulamite [Song of Songs] – and then realised she should have said Shunammite, the woman who looked after Elisha[4] – so I had a very enjoyable time interpreting the Song of Songs and putting flesh on that lovelorn creature – and I think the ladies enjoyed it too!

Sadly, women's meetings as they were even ten years ago are a dying breed, yet there are still so many people of my generation and those before and after me who miss them, not only for the fellowship and cups of tea, but for the spiritual stimulation they received each week. And those who couldn't get enough would join every such meeting in town! This book is for them – to help make up for what has been lost in the name of progress; but it is also for the earlier, younger generations whose work and family commitments prevented taking time out, and who maybe didn't know the value of what they were missing.

I have ended each chapter with a short thought or prayer, followed by a reflection that ties in either directly with the subject or with the over-all theme of that section.

While, despite its title, *Advent Women* can be read at any time of the year, Advent is a very good time to take a fresh look at these women's stories, their ethos, their exploits - not as 'lessons' to be learnt or 'examples' to follow, but as challenges to us in our own situations to be more venturesome, more courageous in the outworking of our faith, to be given a voice, and to do some new thing for God.

WOMAN

I am The Woman.
I stand before you, waiting
to be acknowledged.

1: EVE: WOMAN INCARNATE

Genesis 2:18-4:2a

Advent is waiting - waiting for incarnation, for God. There is a sense in which Eve herself is an incarnation - the first woman - a woman created as part of a man yet distinct from him - and created, as has been suggested, not from a rib but from Adam's side - making her quite literally, his 'other half.' Edith Deen, a writer specialising in Biblical women, declares that, 'The fact that God did not give man dominion until he had woman standing beside him is evidence enough of her exalted place in the Creation.'[5]

A woman with a mind and will of her own?

Or was she?

Made for each other, for companionship, they were contented - even though the norms of the day were written into the relationship, making her subservient. She became, as one put it, 'a convenient peg on which men have hung unflattering theories about women.' She has even been referred to as 'an afterthought of the Maker.'

The text and its interpretation have led to great arguments among Christians (and others) of all persuasions – the fact that the woman is supposed to be the servant of the man because the Bible distinctly says, 'God brought her to the man.' The counter-argument suggests, however, that even though the woman was given to the man as a 'helpmeet', and that wives have rendered valuable service to their husbands in every field of human activity in every period of the world's history, she was, nevertheless, not created solely to be his subordinate, at his beck and call in every situation, even if that view still holds in many parts of the world. Certainly John Milton didn't seem to agree with that idea when he wrote ...

> *O woman, best are all things as the will*
> *Of God ordained them; His creating hand*
> *Nothing imperfect or deficient left*
> *Of all that He created, much less man.*[6]

Far from it. Adam and Eve's relationship is presented as an idyllic marriage, blessed by the Creator God who looked over them.

But not for long. Within that perfect garden rebellion was brewing. The serpent was a wily creature with an insidious nature that began to vie for power - the kind of power given to Adam which made him Adam's property. How to usurp that? Simple. Through his most precious possession - the woman. What follows is the most well-known incident in Eve's life, where her example is not one to be followed. It is hard to condemn her, given the number of women in the world today, even in the churches, who have entered into temptation because the tempter was beautiful, subtle and beguiling. Really? This is where studying the situation opens our eyes.

A group of Sunday School children were asked how they visualised the serpent, and with one voice they answered, "A snake!" One young lady of ten even produced her Children's Bible with a picture of a snake appearing from a bush just to prove that her teacher was "all wrong." Folklore had decreed that the final state of this creature was all there was of him, with no thought that it was in that form as a result of its own wrong-doing, since nothing on the earth had been created ugly. It didn't seem to occur to them that had he been other than charming to her Eve would never had listened, looked where he pointed, and been tempted by that delicious-looking fruit – which of course their Children's Bible depicted as a rosy red apple!

But why did the serpent choose Eve rather than Adam, the supposed dominant human? Was it because it believed her to be the most intelligent, the most ambitious - or the most gullible of the two? And this was a period when there was no natural enmity, so instigating a conversation with her was easy.

"What did God say about eating the fruit?"

Eve had the instructions off pat. Anything but that one tree. If they ate that it would kill them.

Did she at that point understand death? Was it some instant annihilation, or the slow lingering process we have come to know?

"Rubbish!" was the tempter's response. "You won't die - you will become independent, have eyes and minds of your own, and be able to distinguish good things from bad."

Was it a sudden thirst for knowledge that made Eve look at the tree in a new light? Now it wasn't something that was taboo but something that held promise, that looked attractive and good for food.

Did Eve want the wisdom the fruit offered, or simply the fruit for itself, because it looked so good? The desire to be wise has dominated history. No one wants to be or to appear to be ignorant.

That's what education is all about - to make us wise, give us understanding, equip us for life ...

Eve wanted all these things - for herself, her husband, her unborn children ... and if what the creature said was true, only resisting a piece of fruit stood in her way.

Placed in this situation, it has been argued in her defence that far from being weak, deceitful, ambitious or just inquisitive, she was **daring.** Adam wouldn't have had the courage. He didn't even try to stop her! There is no suggestion that he even attempted to argue with her. He just stood there and watched the headstrong woman send the whole world to work, and when he realised she was safe, he took the fruit she offered him and willingly ate it.

Eve was a pioneer. In a sense, as first woman, she could be nothing else. She had so much potential that she hadn't recognised. Now, in that one act, she discovered the extent of her power, not least over her husband.

Sadly, though, it was power misused.

Eve has been credited with turning all women over to a life of suffering through childbirth and parenting - but is that strictly true? Sooner or later even the perfect couple in Paradise would have parented children and physically there could have been no difference. Pain is a reality of both birth and death.

There is also the suggestion, which Milton is at pains to demonstrate, that the two could not have lived together satisfactorily if Adam had not given in to her – it had to be a partnership of equals.

But in reality Eve has been turned by Hebrew historians from being a partner in God's work to becoming a servant - a slave almost. They could not afford to portray her as anything but subservient, and in many cultures today, where sons are counted as treasure, an insurance policy for old age, women are regarded as little more than child-bearing machines, to be exposed at birth if they arrive in inconvenient numbers. Little thought seems to be given as to how these children are to be cared for when their parents live in dire poverty and material want.

And those learned interpreters of scripture didn't stop there. Here was a woman who, caught with the fruit as though she had stolen it, blamed (rightly) the serpent, just as Adam had blamed her (unjustifiably so, as he didn't **have** to take it).

The serpent got a raw deal, and deserved it.

Adam and Eve suddenly gained a new consciousness of one another. Before this Adam had seen her and thought her 'good to look at,' the only hint of her looks in the Bible. She is assumed to have been 'the Most Beautiful woman the world has ever known,' as one writer put it, and while some have attempted to provide a more realistic image for her, the majority of writers and especially artists have depicted her in terms of what was considered beautiful in their age and place. Hardly surprising, of course, when she was the prototype and the possibility of disfiguring disease had only arrived the minute Eve ate the fruit.

Eve's education had begun, though the pair paid a high price - expulsion from Paradise and welcome to a world that was harsh and unforgiving. But, unlike the serpent, she was not cursed. Instead she was to learn that God supplies the basics of life (and would give her the skills that would keep them clothed and fed thereafter). But she learned other lessons, too.

And one of these was the lesson of faith, of trust in the God she had disobeyed yet who had forgiven her.

For Eve, whose name meant 'life giver', the beginning of wisdom lay in the very act of misappropriating it - and maybe that was not the tempter's intention. When her sons were born she acknowledged God's part in these miracles of new life - even in her pain. Perhaps that was the very situation that convinced her that God had not finished with them altogether, but was giving them a new and more fulfilled life, despite the loss of their original 'home comforts.'

When we consider what we in the twenty-first century have to assist us in the process of childbearing, the medical care, preparatory classes, helpful books, etc., how we may shudder to think of poor Eve bearing all the pain and uncertainty alone, with no one to reassure her. All we have on record are these words, put so quaintly in the AV, "I have gotten a man from the Lord." An exclamation of sheer wonder.

Perhaps the most poignant verse in this whole reading is the first in Chapter Four, the time when we really think about God's gifts to humankind. In the account of the birth of Eve's first child Scripture is very sparse, very blunt. There are no details, no hints of the accompanying emotions, and there must have been many, yet here she was, the first woman bearing the first child, an experience none could have told her about, an event no one was able to prepare her for. Rather, she 'worshipped' Cain, whose name meant 'to get' or 'to possess.' Abel, on the other hand, is 'a breath ... a vapour' - 'doomed to fade.' Were those names prophetic, even then? The Hebrew religion came to set great store by the meanings of names.

Did she, one asks, see her favourite first-born branded with shame, while the pitiful Abel became a martyr? Here she becomes a clear warning to parents not to have favourites. Abel is presented as 'insubstantial, ephemeral, futile. A Nobody. So did she mourn his death, or the loss of Cain when he had to run away? She had yet to learn – if she ever did – that, thankfully, 'God cares about the Nobodies.'

Perhaps the fact that Eve was so alone in birthing made her an inadequate parent, and created in her an imbalance in her relationships with her children. She had, after all, never been a child herself! Or had she? At least one commentator has compared that state of pre-fall innocence akin to childhood? Adam and Eve, two children growing up in the garden, learning lessons. 'They have not been able to resist the delights of playing on the railway lines of Eden,' wrote Trevor Dennis. 'Now they have learned their lesson ...'[7]

So is Eve worthy of our Advent recollection? Worthy of the position of Woman Incarnate? A woman who succumbed to the temptation to be wise, which taught her sharply the lesson of good vs. evil, but who instead of nursing resentment for what was lost, recognised God's hand in her life and could still do so even through the pain of giving birth.

Writing to Timothy, Paul attacks women. They, not men, were the transgressors. He hadn't worked out the fact that Jesus had actually emancipated women by keeping company with them, caring about them, healing them, and even teaching them. Or perhaps it suited him not to look too closely at Jesus' relationship with them!

Unlike the many others we read of in the Bible, we can only see Eve as a prototype of humanity as it is, fallen, yet full of potential for life. Eve means 'Life.' She has been seen on a par with a Shakespearean character in whom we can recognise our own mother. Advent looks forward to life, to incarnation. Eve has set the pace, realistically. Though 'ordained man's companion,' she has in a sense become the leader, giving 'the tone to human life,' as one writer, Robert F. Horton, suggests. He adds that he does not think that Milton has done her justice! 'The decisive lesson ... is not that woman leads man into sin, but that for good or evil, she leads him ...'[8] And the fact that he is so easily led leads to his being branded, in some eyes, as the weaker sex!

However, that is a far cry from the poor Indian woman described by a missionary on furlough some years ago. When it was time for her baby to be born she set off with her husband on foot to the hospital, many miles away, he, in typical fashion, striding ahead. But when he arrived at the hospital and looked round, she was nowhere to be seen. She had had to stop off on the way to give birth! In her own way she was a woman in the line of Eve, for she had had to have the courage to see this thing through alone, in her own immense strength.

Advent Woman not only has the courage to cope alone. She has the will and determination not to be downtrodden, but to draw alongside and help to direct the way in that partnership called marriage.

EVE

Who am I, Lord?
Am I Eve, the one tempted into disobedience?
The captain who led her followers into danger?
The one for ever branded
as bringing sin into a perfect world,
and then presented by artists as perfect woman
as they manicure my imperfections?

Who is there to compare me with?
I am too soon for the Obedient Mother –
she who had no choice but to obey.
I found the freedom to disobey,
yet that freedom bound me
and all my progeny.
Yes, even as the obedient one drew so close to God
to bring His offspring into birth,
so my disobedience drove a wedge between us,
creating all the conflicts earth's history has known.

I am not proud of it.
Yet I retain my own will and determination to succeed,
to make my presence felt,
but so unevenly throughout the world
that Adam still holds dominion in.

> Lord, help me to be free to be
> what I am meant to be –
> not slave, but willing servant
> for your Kingdom's sake.

2: ADAH AND ZILLAH: ARCHETYPAL WOMEN

Genesis 4:16-24

It isn't often in that early patriarchal society that women are named, so to suddenly come across these two makes an impact.

One of the great facetious objections to the creation story is, "Where did Cain's wife come from if the earth began with two people and their two sons, one of whom was killed by the other?" This is a failure to see any early Bible characters as archetypes. The names Adam and Eve, *'ish* and *'isha*, mean just that: man and woman – in no particular quantity.

So their story begins as Cain goes off to settle in another country, presumably populated independently of the Hebrew God and therefore of little account in its history. The birth of Cain's son Enoch leads to the first Biblical genealogy, until, four generations later, Lamech appears, together with his two wives who are specifically named. Why?

Because, as the account unfolds, brief as it is, we see that their relationship with their husband is pivotal to the narrative – but so also is their relationship with their sons.

Firstly, however, who were they? What do we know of them? One theory suggests they may have been sisters, which would account for Lamech marrying both of them (as Jacob later married Leah **and** Rachel because of convention, even though he only intended to marry Rachel, the younger). It is not beyond the bounds of possibility that they could even have been twins – yet they were very different in many ways. Adah is described in terms one might associate with a 21st century fashion icon, a fairly useless adornment who sits painting her nails, as one contemptuous writer put it, while her counterpart might be working her fingers to the bone! Not, one might think, the kind of wife an apparently tough man like Lamech would have chosen!

Zillah, on the other hand, is presented as the one who stayed in the background, a shadowy form who just got on with what was required of her – the practical kind – a bit like the Martha and Mary situation. But together they probably made a good team, loved and respected equally by their husband.

Having two wives was not illegal – and nor was it for the most part throughout the Old Testament, though some commentators would prefer to play down that aspect of the relationship. They were unfortunate enough to be the first such couple to be mentioned.

Their story centres round an incident where Lamech appears to have got into a fight in which, having been wounded himself, he ends up killing his assailant – whether deliberately or accidentally is unclear.

What is clear is that it leaves him distraught, but rather than share it with his male counterparts he takes the unprecedented step of telling his wives, whom he obviously considered worthy of his trust and had no will to keep anything from them, especially given possible repercussions. For this act, rather than laud him for his trust in their intelligence and integrity, he is largely castigated by those who have specialist knowledge of the protocols of the period. His words emerge as threats of vengeance, though to whom is unclear, because he knows that the curse put on his ancestor Cain could be visiting him and he is afraid. In this, it is said, he is making his wives complicit. Rather than raising their profile he is demeaning them, encompassing them in his threats, "stripping them of their womanly dignity," as one critic harshly puts it.

But isn't it really all bluster and self-defence? He needs to be believed, to be supported, and who better than those closest to him? We can only conjecture what their reaction was, but it would certainly be a challenge to them to find the strength to cope with the situation, and it is hard to believe they would condemn him, or feel besmirched by what he'd done. They could well have been only too glad to be kept in the loop, to understand and defend him if enemies came looking for vengeance. It was their time to shine rather than to be diminished – to become the kind of wives other women might take courage from. They were 'firsts' in their marital situation. They certainly don't appear to be the 'naturally timid' women one biased writer thinks they should have been!

But that isn't their whole story, even if it defines their pivotal role in the family unit. What kind of mothers were they, and how much influence did they have over their children? Again there are polar opposites in the family.

As to their qualities as mothers, the sheer emphasis on those sons suggests they had a lot of influence. Their insight and understanding of their children from birth is evident in the prophetic names given to them. Adah's son Jabel (his name meaning 'stream') grew up to be a man of simple tastes – a tent-dweller (more commonly referred to as bedouins today), keeper of cattle – and where cattle and tents are, there has to be water.

Adah's other son Jubal's name meant 'sound' or 'music' and this became his forte, despite his critics and those who looked down on him. One rather sarcastic comment declared that Jubal's only children were 'his harp and his organ.' In other words, he was a useless playboy, considered as having contributed nothing to the furtherance of the race and is of no importance to the general economy. Perhaps Jubal was encouraged in his love of music and his instrumental accomplishments because, as David was to discover many years later, music could have a calming, healing effect on stressed human beings.

Zillah's son, Tubal-cain followed his father and became the engineer of his day, a smith and welder, fashioning and inventing artefacts from metal, sadly, including weapons which ended up being used more for destruction than for building anything.

Between them they were founders of three groups – the outdoor shepherd/farmer/countryman, supplier of food, on whom survival depended; the musician, the arch-culturist, for music was to become important in the transmission of their story; and finally, the metal-workers who would fashion the equipment needed by the farmers for the work of digging and planting, many of the musical instruments used, and in due course, weapons of warfare. This last achievement may have bearing on the incident in which the women had become embroiled. Had Lamech begun to put his trust in the weapons of Zillah's son rather than in God? And did Zillah ever question the 'base use made by her husband of their son's invention?'

All three sons in turn had families of their own who continued the traditions of their fathers. Zillah also had a daughter, **Naamah**, meaning 'pleasant' and it could be that she saw in that child all the things she herself had not been, and ensured for her all the things she had been denied, for it rather seems that she was Leah as opposed to Adah's Rachel. The very fact that she is named (as Leah's daughter Dinah was) indicates that Naamah too was a special woman in her time, and like her mother and aunt, owning a place of importance in the life of family and community, co-equal with the men.

But is it right to consider Adah and Zillah as Advent Women in the context of the influence of their sons to future generations rather than their own influence on and activities in the wider family?

Looking ahead, surely the answer to that question lies with the Advent Mother herself, the one who gave birth to and nurtured the son who was to become so much more than any before him – the Son of God sent to bring salvation to the whole world.

These two are the A to Z of womanhood, the equivalent of the feminine alpha-omega – all women, the arch-types – not women to be kept down or deceived, but women sure enough and respected enough to be told the truth, regardless of the consequences. They are indeed Advent Women, women in one sense before their time, yet in another urged along by it.

The Genesis narrative moves on to Adam's line through Seth, but at each phase we read 'sons and daughters' and see how both are respected and pivotal in the furtherance of the race.

COMMUNITY

Lord God, Great Gift-Giver,
You create in us varying abilities –
all of which contribute to the balance of community life.
Some may be the inheritors of Jabel –
shepherds, lovers of nature, workers in the land,
or of Jubal, the music-maker,
bringing joy and pleasure into drab lives.
Yet others are the artisans, the progeny of Tubal-cain,
whose talents may be used for good or ill –
May they be tempered by his sister's pleasantry –
the soothing touch, the gracious word.

Lord God, in Your scheme of things
all these are one, equal, indivisible,
for You create communities
intent on breeding peace
not discord, discontent and rivalry.
No one is disregarded, or demeaned –
You made a perfect world.

3: ABRAHAM'S WOMEN: USED OR ABUSED?

Genesis 11:26–12:20; 15:1–18:15; 20:1–21:20; 23:1-20

Think of Abraham, think of Sarah. Think of Sarah and forget the other women whose lives her husband touched. In the Biblical record there are at least three, and one of these takes up more space in Genesis than even the account of creation.

We go back to Terah and his three sons, one of whom, Haran, died young, but not before fathering a child, Lot, by an unnamed, unmentioned wife. The others are more fortunate – **Sarai and Milcah**, the daughters of another Haran, distinguished by being named also as the father of Iscah. At this point Milcah drops out of the picture, leaving Sarai, distressed by her barrenness.

Terah, it seems, had set out to reclaim Canaan, but got as far as a place he called Haran, presumably named after his dead son. There he settled, along with his family and his grandson, Lot, until he died.

At some point God ruffled Abraham's feathers and told him he had to complete the journey his father had begun, and so he went, taking with him his wife, his nephew 'and the persons they had acquired,' leaving a comfortable life in a stone house for one in goat's hair tents!

And among those 'acquisitions' would have been Lot's own wife, and maybe even his daughters, though no mention is made of them at this juncture. Later, when Abraham rescues Lot from foreign envoys the same language is in use – 'and the women' with his goods.

But it is Sarai/Sarah, whose story begins around 2200 BC in what we now term the Bronze Age, who is most abused, because she is beautiful and Abraham is a coward.

What kind of man would deliberately try to pass his wife off as his sister, with all the possible attendant moral dangers, just to save his own skin? Was she the first recorded victim of domestic abuse? She has been named as the first **obedient** woman in Scripture. Though she did lose her temper a couple of times, she was never disobedient. But perhaps that obedience went more than a little too far. Even Martin Luther reputedly said that if he wanted an obedient wife he would have to carve her out of marble!

Without wishing to wax lyrical one might well ask how Sarai felt as she was taken away by the Egyptians and deposited in Pharaoh's harem. Scared out of her mind – or thankful to be away from her tyrant of a husband? Some writers have said she was as weak as her unbelieving, fearful husband. Even though, according to Eastern custom, women could only be addressed through their husbands, because of Abraham's pretence Sarai could have spoken for herself. Had she carried loyalty too far and lost her sense of value? We don't even get a hint of resentment at the constant upheaval and travelling she was subjected to.

The situation, however, is not altogether clear-cut because the ancient documents that formed the source of the Biblical narrative don't agree on her relationship to Abraham. Yes, she was his wife – but she could also have been his sister – or even his step-sister. For them the importance was marrying into the 'clan' and the nature of any previous relationship was unimportant. Nevertheless, that does not excuse deceit.

Did Abraham feel no guilt when he found himself so well treated because the Pharaoh had a new plaything? How did he envisage this lie of his would end? If she had had no scruples about repudiating her husband, she would, nevertheless, have been powerless to do so. Some like to think that it was Sarai herself who revealed the relationship between them, but that is not what the Bible says. Egypt at the time of Abraham was a highly moral and civilised land. Sarai was no saint. In Philistia she was too compliant and suffered indignity for it: the king, however, was a gentleman! Pharaoh had even paid Abraham the bride price for her!

This was one of the rare moments in the Bible – and certainly the first – when God valued the life of a woman so highly that He intervened – to such an extent that when the truth was known, Abraham could well have lost his life.

Abraham is becoming an unlikeable character – the man who has everything, except an heir, unless Lot is counted as such, though he too was rich – and eventually they parted company and Abraham found himself in the harsh terrain of Canaan while Lot chose the luscious plain of Jordan, and settled near the city of Sodom.

Meanwhile, Abraham had been forgiven and was in favour again – but Sarai was still childless – and now his likely heir is named as a servant, Eliezer. God says otherwise, Abraham believes, but he is fickle and soon begins to doubt – and so a covenant is made.

It seems that Sarai is even more faithless and tries to take matters into her own hands in an act that has been described as a 'suicidal sacrifice' born of pride. So, enter **Hagar**, the surrogate mother – yet another abused woman.

Abraham could have refused Hagar. His acceptance was one more sign of weakness and infidelity. A son at any price!

The fact that Hagar conceived also confirmed that the inability to have children lay squarely with Sarai, and now the conflict between the women begins.

Sarai, the woman abused, now becomes the abuser. She recognises her wrong-doing, and then heaps sin on sin by inciting Abraham to take her part and give permission for Hagar's ill-treatment. She is well-described as the 'mother of mischief.'

No wonder the girl ran away!

But Hagar was not being punished by God, despite the fact that she was not herself wholly guiltless, for she did flaunt herself in front of Sarai as soon as she knew she was pregnant. Though He made Hagar return to her mistress because she was legally still bound to her, nevertheless, He was gracious and merciful, and showed compassion on her predicament – and it was Hagar who saw a vision of God's glory!

Even in the Old Testament God was on the side of abused and used women, and in no sense was He holding their sins against them in the way many male writers have portrayed Him. Hagar became a woman fulfilled and recognising God's hand in her life. The exchanges between God and Hagar comprise the most substantial dialogue between God and a woman in Scripture. Inevitably she has been castigated for not choosing a God-fearing wife for Ishmael! It doesn't seem to have crossed her critics' minds that she did not have much of a choice, and wasn't it, after all, natural for her to go home? They also don't seem to pick up on the fact that she is the **only** woman in the Bible to have directly chosen a wife for her son – but such knowledge might have made their criticism even more severe! Hers is the original one-parent family!

Significantly, the prophecy surrounding Ishmael's birth has a chill ring to it today.

Citing another writer, Phyllis Trible, Trevor Dennis has put Hagar's plight into modern terms. She was ...

'three times oppressed ... the faithful maid exploited, the black woman used by the male and abused by the female of the ruling class, the surrogate mother, the resident alien fleeing from affliction ... the pregnant young woman alone, the expelled wife, the divorced mother with child, the shopping bag lady ... the homeless ... etc.' [9]

There is also a strong belief in some quarters that Hagar was actually Pharaoh's daughter, but that seems highly improbable because she could have gone straight back to her father and persuaded him to wreak havoc on Abraham and punish Sarai. This may have arisen because it is thought that Hagar had been given to Sarai as a maid when she was taken into Pharaoh's palace and had stayed with her.

But God hadn't finished with Sarai, now to be known as Sarah. There would be a blessing even for her – and that blessing would be encapsulated in the gift of a son. Abraham greeted this news with a fit of laughter and a torrent of disbelief. Despite this, God set out to keep His promise – but on the day the three messengers arrived to confirm it, it was Sarah who laughed – and then denied it. Hadn't Abraham prepared her for this news, or had his own disbelief drummed such an action out of him? He should have been doing his part to bring the promise to fruition, but had failed God by denying his wife. He was far too busy involving himself in the destruction of Sodom and Gomorrah and once more (if the editing is to be believed) attempting to pass Sarah off as his sister this time at Gerar, to King Abimelech. But a strange thing happened there. As long as she was there no one in the king's household became pregnant! Enough of a marvel in itself to raise questions!

How undeserving Abraham was, both of God's trust and Sarah's loyalty.

But was Sarah any better when jealousy consumed her at the sight of two innocent children playing together, as brothers would do? Some would cite shades of Cain and Abel but that was probably farthest from Sarah's mind.

And again, seventeen years after the first time, Abraham had the task of dismissing the unwanted slave – albeit technically his second wife. Again she becomes the victim, and again, as she despairs of her son's life, God seeks her out, provides for her, and gives her His assurance – and the faith of Hagar far surpasses that of God's covenant people. But what an irony to find that in the writer of the Hebrews' list of those with outstanding faith, Sarah's name is at the top of the league! And with such an audience this was no political correctness! Was the writer unaware of the facts – or was he varnishing the truth to make his point by appearing inclusive – a rare thing even in the early church?

Sarah died at 127 years, the only woman in the Bible whose age at death is recorded, but was it through age and weariness, or was it because of something else? The suggestion has been made that Sarah died from shock at the news that Abraham had taken Isaac into the mountain to be sacrificed, before the counter-news that God had intervened had been relayed to her. It is a fanciful thought, because it is generally understood that Isaac would have been much younger – and there is nothing to suggest that he was not still about when she died.

Whenever it happened, and despite everything, Abraham mourned – yet wished to 'bury his dead out of his sight' – and even that couldn't be achieved without haggling with Ephron the Hittite for a cave at Machpelah.

But was that the end? No. As custom dictated, Abraham decided where a wife for Isaac should come from, and when that was settled he married again, despite his advanced age.

Is there something sinister in the terminology 'took a wife'? Generally speaking, women had very little say in those days, so was **Keturah** another abused woman, forced into a marriage with an ancient patriarch, increasing his descendants by yet another six sons? Perhaps trying to preserve Abraham's credibility.

Added to that we are told that he also had concubines – and not only one, for the term is plural. Had Keturah herself been his concubine? That is not what the Genesis account says, but in 1 Chronicles 1:32, she is described as a 'slave woman' which may be designed to explain why all their children were given gifts before being sent away. Isaac alone would inherit.

Is this in some way a criticism of their polygamous society? Time and again God promised Abraham's future through the child of one woman – his legal wife. But even in old age it seems the man wasn't satisfied. Ten grandsons by Keturah are named – the unnamed can only be guessed at. Whatever he had, he'd wanted more. Had he had power to look to the future and see that one of those sons would become father of the Midianites who sold Joseph to the Ishmaelites, how then would he have reacted? (One might also question whether these dealers were even aware of the relationship between them?)

But in death, at the age of 177, one encouraging thing happened – Isaac and Ishmael shared the burial, recognised and recognising, and in a sense vindicating both mothers, though maybe even in death Sarah would have rejected the very woman she thrust on Abraham, through her own guilt. And yet, if we compare these two women, we can't but agree that the one who best encapsulates God's relationship with womankind is Hagar – for she could boast no self-sufficiency. At death's door, lost in a desert, she threw herself completely on God's mercy and tasted the fruits of His compassion, provision and His strength that enabled her to keep going and have hope for the future. This was Advent Woman, having no need of a man for her salvation, but recognising her total need of God. If we're only reading the Bible looking for examples, then here she is. I have a lot of time for Hagar!

It is a tangled tale, yet from it we see women who became the precursors of all abused women. One man's greed and lack of faith affected the lives of three named women and possibly numerous unnamed ones. Two at least rose above their situation, though there was no unity between them. The other saw her children rejected and sent away, not even party to their father's burial. Keturah, it seems, was a wife of convenience, nothing more.

Advent, season of incarnation, reminds us that family life should be founded on love, not on violence, hatred and jealousy – and that all are equal in God's sight and that none should be abused or treated unjustly.

INTERACTION

Our lives are not lived in a vacuum,
we don't reside on our own private desert islands –
therefore we co-exist with others,
our lives touch theirs and theirs ours.
We may harm or help,
and we may suffer hurt.
We may abuse or affirm
and we may ourselves be used.
We must not live to and for ourselves
but for others.
We need to be the word and works of God for others
and we need to recognise Him
in those whose paths we travel or cross.
There must be no deceit, no subterfuge among us,
but openness and honesty
for all must be safe in our company.
We need to be so close to our Parent God
that our lives are not only touched by His
but known and seen to be so,
for we cannot live to self
when we live for Him
and He lives in us.

4: REBEKAH: THE FREE THINKER

Genesis 24:1-67; 25:19–27:46

From earliest times in the Middle East and Asia, marriages have been arranged. Any wife would not do. She had to have background, an impeccable pedigree, a dowry, social standing, good blood. Good looks were a bonus – the man would always get the best deal.

For the woman it was a different matter and she would be quite likely to find herself the young bride of some old man like Abraham, bent on increasing his lineage.

When it came to a wife for Isaac Abraham was taking no chances. Accepting that he was too old to travel himself, he sent that old servant who at one time he assumed would inherit his estate.

It was an onerous task and the seriousness of it was impressed on him by the oath he was compelled to make. However, the servant was also a realist. "What if ... What if she didn't want to?" But surely the question was unheard of! Women had no right to refuse – had they?

Perhaps not to the marriage, but going to a foreign country with a strange servant was a different thing altogether. Abraham was realistic too. On no account was Isaac to leave him, but the servant couldn't compel her if she didn't want to go with him – and would incur no blame.

It must have been a worrying journey. How was he to find the right girl? His heart must almost have failed him when he saw the number of girls on the way to the well – all young, all free, all probably lovely to look at. It was the job of these young women to fetch and carry water for their families.

He hit on an idea. "Suppose I ask one of them for a drink and she even offers to water the camels!"

It was hoping for a lot. Camels are thirsty beasts – and ten of them ...!

But Providence led Eliezer straight to Nahor's grand-daughter, and he immediately knelt and gave her gifts from Abraham's treasure store – which her covetous brother promptly took note of!

Perhaps the sight and sound of the wealth alone would have been enough to persuade them. Their first response was, "Take her and go ..." But by morning they were having second thoughts and pleading for extra time, as families do.

It was then that they did that unprecedented thing of letting Rebekah have the final say in her own destiny – and she didn't hesitate.

She said, "I will!"

She chose to go – exercised her own free will.

Only that's not quite how the Biblical editor records it when he says, 'So they sent away their sister Rebekah and her nurse along with Abraham's servant ...' And a host of maids.

Free-thinker and a woman of observation and intuition. There must have been something about the man in the field who was making his way towards them. She knew, and must have decided there and then that this was her man – and she wasn't going to short-change herself.

Just like that? Perhaps not. After all, Abraham was family, and though far away they hadn't been quite so cut off from news as we might imagine. Camel trains passed from one place to another, messages were exchanged – and the rise of Abraham was no secret, and nor was the child of his old age, now grown to manhood and probably very nearly old enough to be Rebekah's father! Imagine what it would be like to belong to Abraham's dynasty! Not to have to scrimp and save and patch up old clothes, but to be rich – for it was known that he had great wealth in cattle and sheep. Perhaps Rebekah had dreamed these impossible dreams – and suddenly the impossible was happening. She had seen the wealth, received it, witnessed it given to her family as the bride price.

And now she had seen him before he'd had an opportunity to see her. It wasn't done – but she must have liked what she saw. The mystery would be on his side until after the marriage had taken place.

How close had Isaac been to his mother? Too close perhaps! And the act would be even more sharply focused when he realised that Abraham's brother was not her father, but her **grandfather**.

Again, she was 'taken' – but she went willingly and freely and his love for her, genuine and deep, was obviously reciprocated, though the Bible gives no hint of this. Love was not a word outside the vocabulary of even an arranged marriage. And he, if the interpretation of her name is correct, was ensnared, captivated, caught in 'a noose'!

But in even the most perfect matches things don't always go well. Like her mother-in-law before her, Rebekah was 'barren', unable to conceive children.

No doubt this stung Isaac and tested their relationship, but did he learn from his parents' messy lives that there was no need for drastic action? Amazingly, yes. Whereas Abraham had doubted,

Isaac prayed about it, and his prayer was answered. But the answer to that prayer gave Rebekah a hard time.

So she, too, 'went to the Lord.' She wasn't in the business of waiting for someone else to do it, or for God to take the initiative. She asked Him what was going on. And she got her answer.

Twins! Twins vying for supremacy even before birth – tearing her apart in pregnancy as they would in growing up.

The couple made one huge mistake. They each had a favourite son. It may be human nature but it is not good parenting, least of all because Isaac's reason for favouring Esau was more culinary than emotional. He liked his game. Perhaps that was a contributory factor to Jacob's coveting the birthright. Maybe too she had waited so long for children that she didn't view motherhood rationally.

Isaac meanwhile was on the move, just like his father – but did he also share his father's cowardice when he tried to pass Rebekah off as his sister? Possibly his one act of disrespect, discovered when he then forgot himself and gave her a hug! In this deceit he could have not only harmed their relationship but damaged their whole future. Indeed, what has been hailed as an idyllic love story was doomed to disaster, not by his deception, but by her own. In this they were well matched.

Certainly Rebekah's preference for Jacob had its backlash – for Esau deliberately married foreign wives, knowing how upset she would be. **Judith and Basemath** were Hittites.

But Rebekah the free-thinker, far from passive, was also far from perfect, and when the opportunity to get her own back on Esau arose she took it.

Maybe scheming is adjunct to free-thinking, but one overheard conversation was enough to devise a plan to give her favourite the blessing reserved for their firstborn. And not only that; she took upon herself the curse that would rightfully be his if the deceit were discovered. She became a woman with a split personality – one part good, God-fearing, the other devious and cruel, but probably she didn't realise what she really was. It was as though she had snatched control of her own life from God.

Did she also know about the stolen birthright?

At her instigation Jacob incriminated himself and deceived his father. Did he at that moment recall buying Esau's birthright for another meal? He lied through his teeth to please his mother and achieve his end.

How did Rebekah feel when she heard Isaac's words to Esau, "When you break loose you shall break his yoke from your neck?" In encouraging the deception she herself had broken away from tradition, she had allowed her own emotions to overrule her common sense, and in so doing she had put enmity between the two enough to run the danger of her favourite being killed for his crime.

Another ruse was called for – and she found it in the ongoing battle with Esau's Hittite wives.

"I'm fed up with those two," she told her unsuspecting husband (or would it be more appropriate to describe him as gullible?). "It will be the last straw if Jacob also marries one of those local women."

The scheming woman hadn't forgotten her own roots, nor the day she came into Isaac's life. One word to Isaac and she knew he too would remember – and he did.

Jacob didn't have to run from Esau. He was sent, with his father's blessing.

And Esau took note. He had lost yet another blessing and was desperately trying to make up to his father, whose favourite he had been – so he went to Ishmael's family and found another wife, **Mahalath,** Ishmael's daughter.

As though a silent comment on that act, we hear no more about him from then on until the moment the brothers are reconciled years later. An even greater silence descends on Rebekah. Did she, as has been suggested, die of a broken heart at the loss of not one but both sons? Maybe she even lost faith in God – or did she repent of her machinations and realise that, free-thinker that she was, she didn't always make the right choices? No record of life or death exists beyond that point, except in her son who goes on deceiving and extricating himself, despite his allegiance to – or is it patronage by? – God. Maybe Rebekah, knowing God's prophecy about Jacob, really thought she was helping the job along! The fact that Jacob's superiority had been prophesied is no excuse. God can achieve His purposes with honesty and integrity. He doesn't need people to lie and cheat for Him.

Perhaps Rebekah was really a woman before her time, a one-off who placed no rein on the activities of her mind, so that life became as uncomfortable for those whose paths she crossed as Esau's wives were to her. Esau's own eventual willingness to be reconciled spoke the volumes that should have been written from the side of Rebekah, for while Jacob was at that point his own man, she was the one whose thinking muddied the waters.

Advent impresses upon us that being caught up in God's plan is not always to be given the assurance of a comfy ride. Advent Woman will be willing to take risks, to go into the unknown with God, to enable Him to fulfil His own plans through her. But she must not take them into her own hands and in so doing risk working against Him.

📖   📖   📖   📖   📖

CONDITIONS

The Bible contains many examples of people praying – and making conditions,
or tempting God with that old certainty, the 'what if' of circumstances,
the hope of an alternative when the Spirit prompts people against their will.

Abraham, called to sacrifice Isaac, saying, 'I will' – but was it with the hope that God would intervene and send the ram?

And Rebekah, bidden to go with a strange man to marry a distant relative she'd never seen.

Did she say, "Give me time, give me an image of him"? Was she bound by the will of her family? No. The decision had to be hers alone. No consultation with her family, no being like Salome and asking her mother's opinion. (John the Baptist was not the only loser that day.)

No conditions there – a categoric "I will go."

But what of the man she travelled with? ...

"What if ... she refuses ... or I get the wrong girl? How will I know?
I know! I will lay down a condition – it has to be the one who waters my camels!"

Then there was plan B - 'If ...' If Gideon's fleece was wet on a dry night or dry on a wet one ... Repeat. Repeat again!

Conditions can be so limiting.

God created us with eyes and ears – and minds.

He didn't lay down minor conditions to make us obey Him. He asked only two things – "that you trust Me without conditions, and love Me the way you love yourself. Even then you will still have your freedom. I won't stop you saying 'No'. Just don't lay down conditions."

May we who read these stories learn to live in love and trust and have no need to question or make conditions.

5: JACOB'S WOMEN: HONOUR AND DISHONOUR

Genesis 28:1-5; 29:1–31:55; 33:1-3; 34:1-31; 35:16-27

Two wives, two concubines, twelve sons and one daughter – a recipe for family disaster!

The story of Jacob's acquisition of this company is supposed to be one of God's guidance and provision, but it reads like a horror story in places, a grim catalogue of plot and counter-plot, division and deceit.

From his first encounter with Laban there is a sense of treachery. The impression is given that Rachel had grown up in a household where her grandfather, Bethuel, was not respected in his own house. Laban, Jacob's uncle, was in control, making the decisions along with his mother. It almost seems as though this deceitful streak permeated the whole of Terah's descendants. Thus it was that having fallen in love with Rachel's beauty and been promised her as his 'wages', on his wedding night Jacob found himself married to Leah, the plainer older sister. A week later the nuptials were repeated and this time Rachel was his - but again paid for by the next seven years of labour.

Perhaps it was a norm of the times but how did these sisters feel about being 'bought' in the way cattle might be bought at the market? Isaac had told Jacob to 'take a wife' from Laban's daughters. They would have no say in the matter. 'Take' was also not an operative word – Jacob paid a high price for them both. Leah in particular had been 'sold'. Nevertheless, she seems to have had one important asset – faith, a faith that one day her husband would really love her. Most importantly, it is from Leah's descendants that David, Israel's greatest king, arose, from whom Messiah would one day be descended. Had she known it, that was her greatest honour. Jacob's favourite simply couldn't compete! It was in death that Leah would be most honoured, with burial in the family grave.

Then there was the perennial problem of childlessness. Was there something about the lifestyle or the tension surrounding this family unit that created barriers to fertility? It wouldn't be recognised then, but it is now.

Leah knew her place and little mattered, so she didn't suffer from the tension in the way that somehow Rachel did. Rachel knew she was the loved one but that made it all the more imperative that she had children. So, like Jacob's grandmother, she stooped to using **Bilhah**, her maid – just at a time when Leah had stopped having children – so naturally she followed suit with **Zilpah**. But the record makes it plain that even these two were Laban's possessions. No one had a soul to call their own, least of all two servants, deputed to them by Laban on their marriage. How did they feel, having no status except mothering the children of these other women's husband? Used – or abused?

Interspersed with their continued interaction is the constant stream of deceit exercised not only by Laban but by a cunning, clever Jacob whom nothing had changed, and who eventually decided to cut loose without formal permission.

When Jacob later told them he wanted to leave Laban and return home the two put their feelings on the table – what had they to lose? Everything they were and had, even their children, were still owned by their father. Could they be any worse off in a new country owned by their husband? They were not about to stand in Jacob's way.

Their marriage had divided them, brought shades of envy that hadn't previously existed, maybe because they were even then united against their father. Now once more they had a common bond.

To a lot of people reading the story today, Rachel is the heroine while Leah is seen as the villain of the piece. But no one who has studied them in the context both of culture and of their family circumstances, could commend such black and white judgments.

To summarise each one in turn – Rachel, it appears was beautiful, and doubtless in another age she would have had a myriad suitors knocking on Laban's door. She was loved by Jacob at first sight; but because of her childlessness, envious of Leah and therefore determined to get what she wanted – **needed** - by any means, even to giving her maid to Jacob, seeking children by proxy.

Leah, on the other hand, is described as plain, possibly tall and thin, and with poor eyesight, as 'tender eyed' was a way of describing someone with a sight defect. Laban must have despaired of ever getting her off his hands – until love-sick Jacob arrived on the scene, looking for a wife, and he hatched his plan. But it seems she still remained the odd one out – hurt, feeling unloved and unwanted. Imagine what she felt like! It went hard when, in a land where heirs were a necessity, that even after having four sons, Jacob loved her no more than he had ever done. She must have been loyal and patient, bereft of pride, and she must have loved Jacob regardless. It seems she willingly complied with all issues thrown at her – her situation, Rachel's attitude, even to giving up her maid to Jacob when she thought she would have no more children.

But how did they both feel about their husband when, faced with the possible hostility from Esau, he split them into family groups and created a hierarchy that once again set Leah and Rachel at odds? Leah, mother of his first sons, found herself second to the maids, but clearly not in the safety zone. A true hierarchy would have set some acceptable order of importance.

What was it about Rachel that had, in the end, made her appear blessed by God when she seemed to have had so many lapses – envy, covetousness, superstition? As she prayed so fervently for her heart's desire, didn't she feel an even greater burden of need for forgiveness? It seemed that her faith was being tested – and failed at the moment she tried to solve her problem by sending Bilhah to 'service' her husband!

To make matters worse, just as it seemed they were succeeding in getting their freedom, Rachel turned thief and took away her father's household gods. Why?

Was she paying him out for something? Challenging him to live without them and worship Jacob's God? Or hedging her bets, thinking that if God wasn't with them these other deities might help? Weren't they to be some kind of insurance policy for her expected second child?

If so, they failed miserably, for Ben-oni, son of her sorrow, was born before they reached their destination, and she died as he was born – and Jacob wouldn't even allow the name she chose, for it would probably have spoken too much of his own guilt.

He buried her with honour. Life couldn't be the same again – and he wouldn't be able to take her and show her off to his mother (had she even been alive by then, which is doubtful), whose own nurse had also died, though it is hardly clear **when** or whether she was with his company or is this a passing geographical reference? That **Deborah** is named at all demonstrates in what esteem she was held. It is likely that she had not only served as Rebekah's nurse but as nurse to her grandchildren – and perhaps, as she grew older, she had become a substitute grandmother, part of the family. If she had begun as a slave, which is more than likely, she certainly had not ended as one. Her burial place was named 'Oak of Weeping.'

So the names of four more women have been handed down to posterity, not so much in their own right but because they were 'owned' by Israel, the foundation stone of the great Abrahamic nation.

But there was one other woman in Jacob's life – his daughter, **Dinah**, whose story shows up both the value of women and the lack of it.

Wisely or not, she'd gone visiting the neighbours, possibly for the female company she must have found in short supply in Jacob's entourage – and she was accosted and abducted by Shechem, who raped her and then decided he would marry her!

No wonder her brothers (Leah's sons) were angry. 'For such a thing ought not to be done' was putting it mildly.

But was the deceit and slaughter that resulted a bigger crime than the rape? We might expect those ancient societies to think so but this chapter, brutal as it is, actually gives to a woman more respect than any other in the Old Testament. Women were bought and sold, an outrage to us. They were possessions, along with the animals and servants, but they were not to be stolen and sexually abused, effectively ruining their lives and prospects. Even in those harsh days of barter and child-bearing machines, women were to be loved and cherished. That Schechem had not only abducted and raped Dinah but imprisoned her in his own house added volumes to his crime which no intercession by his family was about to ameliorate.

What of the girl herself? What choice had she? Any marriage would have been preferable to spending a solitary life as one unfit for sale. That was not the point, though perhaps the despairing Jacob might have thought it a reasonable deal when he heard what his sons had done to the Hivites.

"You have brought troubles on **me** by making **me** odious to the inhabitants of the land." He was concerned only for himself and his own reputation. What about poor Dinah?

"Should our sister be treated like a whore?" Simeon and Levi asked in defence.

Their method may have been wrong but they showed far more respect to their sister than her father did.

The fortunes of Jacob's women depict an Advent-in-waiting for that time of justice and equality that didn't quite seem to touch them.

Advent is about justice, equality and fair dealing for all. It has no place for hierarchy, divisions or violence.

WAITING

Advent is waiting –
waiting for an event,
a moment in history –
in time past, time present,
out of time –
waiting for a coming,
celebrating a past coming,
an anniversary –
a day of peace and joy
set against a tumultuous backdrop
of war, unrest, destruction, desolation –
a world in waiting for another Advent,
the final coming of God into His world –
a world in need of love and justice,
peace and compassion,
a sense of mutual caring,
honesty, openness, equality,
where human life is beyond price,
precious in His sight,
not a commodity to be bought and sold
like antique furniture, rundown warehouses
and de-listed buildings:
a world where wealth must be shared
not gained by treachery,
one in which God's Spirit moves again over the waters
pronouncing all is good.

6. SHARED NAMES: ESAU'S WIVES AND TAMAR

Genesis 26:34-35; 27:46; 28:6-9; 36:1-39; 38:1-30

Women were of little value in those early societies: machines for producing heirs and not much more. Consequently, few are named, but when they are it seems immediately to upgrade their status.

As mentioned, Esau's wives did not descend from the family of Terah, and perhaps that was no bad thing, for the devious deceitful self-seeking streak seemed to permeate every generation.

Unsurprisingly, this did not please Rebekah, who felt it a deliberate ploy to upset her, yet it is quite unlikely that **Judith and Basemath** were ever disloyal to Esau and he obviously did right by them according to their own rules - that is, until he lost his blessing, and then - only then - did the proverbial penny drop that he was displeasing his father.

So what did he do? Went to Egypt and found one of Abraham's other descendants, **Mahalath**, daughter of Ishmael!

Did the Hittite wives, who had obviously been friends before marriage, simply accept Mahalath, or were they jealous or vindictive? We are not told, and it could be that Esau had explained his problem to them.

Nevertheless, they had been loyal and still seemed to stand by him when he lost his legacy.

But how many writers have been keeping records and how well did the reputation of these women come down to us?

For in the genealogy we are told that his wives were **Adah** the daughter of Elon the Hittite, **Oholibamah** daughter of Anah, a Hivite, and **Basemath**, Ishmael's daughter! Earlier texts show Elon's daughter to be Basemath and Judith to be the daughter of Beeri, both Hittites. Which record is correct? It seems that the consensus is that Adah = Basemath, and that Ishmael's daughter was also Basemath, since women sometimes received new names when they were married. However, any link between Judith (a pure Hebrew name meaning 'The praised one') and Oholibamah/Aholibamah, daughter of Anah, are without foundation. That creates an interesting dilemma, especially when another conjecture is that Judith was Aholibamah's second name. That is also the explanation for Mahalath Basemath.

The women are cited again in connection with their children - Adah mother of Eliphaz, who became father of five sons.

Basemath, mother of Reul, who had four sons. Oholibamah had three sons.

Warming to his cause, the narrator then looks into the future and sets Esau's descendants into clans - and each clan has a **mother figure**, one of Esau's wives.

In addition, sisters are sometimes mentioned. Just as Leah's daughter Dinah is named, so is **Timna**, sister of Lotan, one of the Horites in Seil. Timna is also named as a concubine of Eliphaz, and there is obviously significance there, the usual explanation being that they are one and the same, and this Timna had a daughter of the same name.

The account then goes on to list the kings of Edom (Esau's land) until the name of Hadar, king of Pua, is named - and his wife, **Mehetabel**.

Why are these women so important?

This was a feudal society, where families formed clans and were ruling factions, but while each had an elder or chief, the ones who kept the family together were the mothers. It is just so in many third world countries today.

Is this a sign that contrary to the Israelite situation when the women might be 'power behind', these women were up-front and emancipated - and little wonder, then, that Rebekah's life was made a misery, for they showed up what had been missing in her own relationship. She was expected to be submissive. These women perhaps were freer and not required to be subservient provided they were faithful.

Did this strike a chord of rebellion in Rebekah, or is the supposition following too much on a style line of reasoning?

Whatever, those women had a power unthought of in Hebrew households, but it was exercised in such a way that they retained and gave the respect of their husbands, while Rebekah appears to have lost respect for her husband, only appealing to him when something was beyond her jurisdiction.

Wise mothers don't have to be scheming like Rebekah, or to be doormats, put upon like slaves. Motherhood is not a status to be discarded in the name of feminism (otherwise, why would so many single women with no desire to marry still hanker after children?) It is a responsibility which gives status through the lives of children who follow their good example.

The narrator continues into the next generation of Israel, and the affairs of Judah and his family. It is not clear whether his Canaanite wife or her father was named **Shua**, but the wife of his eldest son chosen by Judah, certainly is.

This is **Tamar** whose successive husbands were dishonourable to the point of death. The custom was that a childless widow could be married to successive brothers until she had a child, regardless of how demeaning it was to the woman concerned.

Having lost two husbands, Tamar is promised the third when he is of age, and sent back to her father, where she remains, blameless, as a widow.

But Judah does not keep his promise, so when his wife dies, she deceives him by posing as a prostitute, and he, to his shame, succumbs with pledges he is unable to give when he can't find her again. It is a one-sided relationship: he can do as he pleases. When he discovers Tamar is pregnant he immediately condemns her to death - but she is vindicated when she produces the evidence against him.

'She is more righteous than I.' He had not kept his promise about his third son. She had sought a future. He had only sought a few fleeting moments of worldliness, and then condemned her for appearing to do likewise.

But saying that she was 'more righteous' than Judah is not saying that she was in any way without blame, and some commentators are adamant that her place in the genealogy of Christ is offensive and accuse her of leading Judah into adultery - but how could she have done that since he was by that time widowed? It is a purist reaction against the presence in Christ's lineage of foreigners, ignoring the fact that it demonstrates how all-embracing God's love really is.

The Bible is far more generous to her than these prudish commentators. While the story of Tamar playing the harlot is familiar, the truths behind it may not be so. She was seeking her rights according to the Law, albeit outside it in some respects, and the Bible distinctly commends her for this. However, even today some find this morally abhorrent, like interweaving Christ's lineage with what they see as degrading to him. But is it? If so, maybe we, and they, have missed the point. Jesus invited those without sin to be the first to throw stones at the adulteress, but no one could. The Apostolic Fathers made a big issue of Jesus' sinlessness and miraculous conception, 'free from taint of original sin,' but they missed the point about Tamar: a sinner for whom Christ died, a maligned wife whose interests Christ would have had very much at heart; and what is more, a Gentile, to demonstrate that all were indeed one in him.

So Tamar, too, became a mother of two future dynasties. The mothers, with the wisdom and sense of justice, were in the most powerful position of influence, even when they were supposedly being kept down, out of sight in the kitchen or the nursery. Their special ministry was - and is - honoured by the Creator.

Advent is centred in the role of motherhood - Elizabeth, Mary - those who were to play leading roles in the Mystery of Incarnation and elevate women's status to new heights.

DESTINY

Is it that the destiny of some is to be subservient?
Rejected by polite society then in the hardness of labour,
hearts harder still,
nursing bitterness.
How different it might have been!
What stroke of fate made one the loser
while all others seemed to win?

Will there be some turning-point, a moment when the truth
confronts them, and they realise that freedom lies
a revolution distant?
Then hope is born:
they are renewed in spirit, rise to fight.
They do not hear the still small voice of reason
urging trust.

7. ISRAEL IN EGYPT: COMMUNITY AND COURAGE

Genesis 39:1-41:57; Exodus 1:1-6:27; 18:1-9; 21:1-22:31; Genesis 46:8-27

Firstly, **Asenath**, daughter of Potiphera, priest of On - Joseph's Egyptian wife, mother of Manasseh ('God has made me forget all the hardship and all my father's house') and Ephraim ('For God has made me fruitful in the land of my misfortune.').

Joseph was not the only one with a foreign wife. Simeon's son Shaul was 'the son of a Canaanite woman'.

From despising foreign alliances, Israel now became wedded to them in every respect. Joseph's rise to power during the years of plenty and of famine brought him an Egyptian wife, Asenath, whose two sons were accepted by Israel, though blessed in reverse order, almost a pattern of his own situation, as if history had to repeat itself.

Jacob himself had been urged by his parents to ensure that his own wife was from pure family stock. How, then, did he educate his own sons in their choice of wives - or did he even, where he could, actually choose wives for them? What is certain is that he was in no position to make any choice for Joseph, whom he had long considered dead and lost. So how did he feel when Joseph turned up as prime minister in Egypt with an Egyptian wife in tow? We aren't told, but he nevertheless accepted Joseph's children. Most people would accept that Pharaoh's gift of a wife went with everything else bestowed on him, and there is no hint that Joseph, who had refused to be led into an immoral liaison with Potiphar's wife, saw any reason not to accept her.

Yet there are those who believe that Joseph **should** have refused to marry her! Why? Perhaps because they saw it as a political arrangement to keep Joseph within bounds, and the fact that she was the high priest's daughter compromised his own religion. We see no such judgment in the Book of Genesis because as far as Joseph was concerned, none was needed. In fact, one modern translation, the Contemporary English Version, says that Pharaoh 'let him marry Asenath', indicating that, with such a high position in the Pharaoh's employ, he would need such permission to marry the priest's daughter. Probably the relationship he had with his own God helped to cement the marriage and make him a good husband. The Bible only highlights such marriages negatively when the wives do lead their husbands away from God (e.g.

40

Jezebel) and there is no suggestion whatsoever that Joseph's faith was compromised or threatened. He knew one thing, that God had saved his life and brought him to Egypt for a purpose, and this was all part of that purpose and she, in a sense, part of God's gift to him for his own obedience.

Years later, however, enmity impressed itself as the Egyptians began to be afraid of the foreigners in their land and to enslave them. Thus came the cue for courage in the form of the two Hebrew superintendent midwives, **Shiprah** ('childbearing' or 'joy of parents') **and Puah** ('prolific' or 'to procreate'). Ancient Jewish historians tell us there were about five hundred midwives in Egypt at that time. Was their response the same as that of Shiprah and Puah?

We may not altogether go along with their reasoning but those two women had far more courage than many men - courage ahead of their time, since what they did was to risk their lives in order to save others.

But faced with an order to kill all new-born boys what else could they do? Courage they had, stomach for the messy business of killing they had not. Their profession involved bringing new life into the world and making sure it lived, not destroying life. Besides, they were very devout women, and they knew in their hearts that this could not possibly be the will of God.

As expected, they were summoned to give account for their disobedience. They had an answer - and how could a 'mere man' dispute it? Hebrew women were tougher than the pampered Egyptians and got on with the birthing business before any midwife arrived on the scene!

True? Or false? It didn't matter to them. It wouldn't even have mattered to them if they had known that centuries later they would actually be accused of cowardly sin because they had not told the truth. They had done what was right in their eyes and were blessed by God because of it, not only keeping their jobs and their heads, but being given families of their own, which assured them of double respect among their own people. One commentator was a little more generous towards them and saw their reply as 'partial truth', labelling them as the ur-anti-abortionists.

Pharaoh had to think of a way to destroy the Hebrews without their help. What is amazing in one way is that he chose to destroy the boys but let the girls live - yet in how many cultures, even today, would it be the girls that were destroyed?

Was it that the girls made better slaves, or that they were seen as suitable wives for the Egyptians, whereas the men would not be allowed near an Egyptian woman? So far removed from Joseph and his Egyptian wife, they had reinstated all their cultural and religious taboos. Or was it simply that girls were not perceived as a threat?

However, he reckoned without the resourcefulness of some Hebrew mothers – one in particular.

Amram and his wife **Jochebed,** a Levite couple, had a son and kept him hidden away till he got too big. Then she put him in a waterproof basket and sent him down the river, knowing full well that he could be floating to his death and she could have blood on her hands and his life on her conscience.

Was it that she would rather he died that way than be killed by Egyptian soldiers? Or was it some quirk of faith that prompted her to take such drastic action?

But what if an Egyptian had found him? Had some instinct already thought of that when she sent her daughter to keep watch?

Jochebed, whose name meant 'God-her-glory' has been described as 'a mother worthy to be ranked with prophets and priests.' This shrewd woman knew when Pharaoh's daughter went to bathe. Moreover, she had watched her and weighed her up, and knew exactly what would happen.

Confidently trusting, she sat at home waiting for her daughter's return and the summons she knew would come: the princess needed a wet nurse - and she could fill the bill.

Plot or Providence? Schemer or a woman so close to God who knew she could trust Him to save her son's life? Through the intensity of her faith she is described as having inherited a vision of what He had appointed for Moses.

And what about the princess who paid her to nurse her own child? Didn't she think it suspicious when this girl appeared from the bushes and offered to find a wet nurse? Or did she turn a blind eye to the truth at the sight of such an appealing child, at the same time marvelling at the resourcefulness of his mother? Was she herself at that point childless?

But what a wrench for the mother when, at two years, she had to sacrifice him to Pharaoh's daughter. That was the price she was willing to pay for her son's life, a life which would give him a privileged upbringing but would eventually challenge him to declare his roots, and at that point it was his adoptive mother who would be left empty and grieving.

For Moses, as the Princess had named him, became a man with a mission, albeit a reluctant one. When he had killed an Egyptian and fled for his life, he was led to Midian, where he was again given shelter in foreign territory - and a wife, **Zipporah**, daughter of the priest of Midian.

Always in these instances it is obvious that wherever they were from, the women had no say in the alliance: Asenath had undoubtedly been **given** to Joseph; the priest **gave** Zipporah, one of his seven daughters to Moses. Zipporah has been described as an Ethiopian, a 'black' woman and certainly that she is no believer in the One God.

So Moses became a father and named his son Gershom, 'for I have been an alien residing in a foreign land.'

But comfortable as he was in his new role, in his heart of hearts he wasn't happy. His people were suffering. How could he ignore them? So it was that when God appeared to him in the mysteriously burning bush his heart was already receptive, even though his mind resisted. He found every excuse under the sun for not doing what God wanted him to do.

Yet in the end he went, and Zipporah went with him - a spirited woman, it seems. We may question the whole episode of why God should test Moses by trying to kill him, unless it is some editorial re-run of Jacob and the angel. But Zipporah's part is puzzling. She becomes, in effect, a healer and a peacemaker, by giving in unwillingly to circumcising Eliezer, their second son, yet the language she uses of Moses is hardly complimentary. In consequence, he sends her back home.

Though it is not clearly specified, Aaron, the brother of Moses, was the eldest son of Amram and Jochebed, older enough to have escaped the Pharaoh's carnage. Aaron's wife also appears to have been a Levite, **Elisheba** (a variant of the name Elisabeth), daughter of Amminadab. Down the line, his son also married into 'the clan' and became father to Phinehas. This, in effect, made her the foundress of the entire Levitical priesthood·

Two other woman are named. **Serah** was the daughter of Asher, a son of Zilpah, whose name meant 'abundance', and **Shelomith** ('peaceful') daughter of Dibri of Dan and an unnamed Egyptian. She had married an Egyptian and their son picked a fight with another Israelite and uttered blasphemy, the penalty for which was death by stoning. Why was this woman named? To shame her because her son was not God-fearing, or because she had married an Egyptian (as had Joseph!)? We aren't even told whether she pleaded for him. The problem had arisen because the Law prohibited him, a 'half-bred', from a place inside the Israelite camp with his mother. If tradition is true, this is not surprising, since his paternity has been attributed to the Egyptian Moses murdered for having killed her Hebrew husband and infuriating her - a theory based on an ancient and somewhat ambiguous Chaldean text.

Perhaps it was a warning that parentage meant nothing when the Name of God was not respected. Shelomith would be the one left bearing the guilt as well as the loss.

Another foreign woman, **Cozbi** ('deception'), a Midianite, was taken by Zimri against the law and killed with him by Phinehas, Aaron's grandson. Guilt does not seem to be ascribed to her so much as to her clan, though it appears that she had been accused of what amounted to witchcraft in 'tempting' Zimri. This, of course, could have been a hangover from past association since Moses had married the daughter of the pagan priest of Midian.

That this execution apparently stemmed a plague of sexually transmitted diseases indicates the seriousness of the situation but killing seems a drastic solution. Was she an unwilling martyr? The matter is an open question. There was a death penalty for many crimes against the person, but when it came to slaves, punishment was less severe - sometimes not at all, for the slave was deemed to be the owner's property.

And sadly, some women, even today, are regarded merely as property, and treated accordingly,

Even rape may be got round by payment and marriage, with, it seems, no consideration for the girl's feelings, only her father's pocket!

The only group of women treated with respect were the widows, perhaps because their status generally left them dependent on charity – and once free of their motherly duties, they were expected to resort to spending their days in virtuous pursuits, or in the temple, living holy lives.

But who, among this plethora of womanhood, stand out as Advent Women – dutiful wives, holy widows – or courageous midwives?

Advent Women may often be found in the background, playing 'bit parts' but the ripples from their lives and actions spread far beyond their own moment.

ENCOURAGEMENT

Covenant God, You plead for us
when we cannot plead for ourselves.
When our spirits are downcast
You come alongside us in encouragement.
When strength fails You go the extra mile for us,
and when the burdens of care press down on us
You help to carry the load.

Forgive us, therefore, when we doubt Your promises,
when we turn our backs on You and try to go it alone.
help us to trust You always to send help and companionship
in the times we need them most -
and to recognise in them that it is **You** who have come to us.

8. PROPHETESSES AND DELIVERERS: MIRIAM, DEBORAH AND OTHER WOMEN OF COURAGE

Numbers 12:1-16; 20:1; Judges 4:1-22; 5:1-31; 9:50-55

Prophets and prophetesses are defined as those raised up by God and inspired by His Spirit to proclaim the will and purpose of God.

Miriam is the first woman in the Bible to be styled a prophetess. Perhaps the distinction came to her simply because belonging to the priestly clan put her in a privileged position, for she was the older sister of Aaron and Moses who, at something between ten and sixteen, had conned Pharaoh's daughter into seeking the help of Moses' own mother to care for him.

What kind of story did that entail? She had lain in wait until the right moment and then just 'happened' on the princess' discovery, brazenly got her into conversation (something that should not have happened between an Egyptian princess and a Hebrew teenager) and then seized her moment. The baby would need a wet nurse and she might know just the person to help - a woman whose child had died or been 'lost' to her, and was sure she'd welcome the opportunity to nurse this abandoned child! It would sound plausible.

Had she inherited the devious family streak? Miriam grew up in Egypt but when they finally escaped she was in the front ranks, with her tambourine, leading the women through the dried-up seabed with a song and poetry as bloodthirsty as her brothers'. By now she is so revered as a prophetess (by her family connections or in her own right?) and as such accepted as a leader, at least of her own kind!

She has attracted a certain amount of over-the-topness, such as being sacred in drama, dance, song, and in sacred instruments, making her worthy to stand out beside her two apparently unapproachable brothers.

Following the account of her activities in reuniting baby Moses with his mother, we hear no more of her until the Israelites have crossed the Red Sea - plenty in fiction, of course, but nothing in fact - until suddenly there she is, now an ageing woman, with her tambourine leading the victory song and given the title 'prophetess'. She is also the first poetess. In his Antiquities, Josephus records that she became the wife of Hur, one of the

Judges of Israel and thus grandmother of Bezalel, artist of the temple. However, the main consensus is that she remained single through her devotion to her brothers and her patriotic nationalism which gave female celibacy a place in Israel's society it had not previously known. This could make her the first woman to be allowed the choice.

Yet Miriam also had a ready tongue and a mind of her own not always in accord with God's. It may also be that at times she was more attracted to Aaron than to Moses and tended to take sides. Was it jealousy? The situation came to a head when she and Aaron objected to Moses' second foreign (Cushite) wife. The poor woman was clearly the innocent party and was caused great pain and injury by Miriam's harsh words. It seemed to her that he was betraying the faith he was supposed to be upholding. It was patriotism *in extremis.*

But was her real sin one of possessiveness? In a very real sense Moses had been her baby, the little brother who still needed her, and now there was this other woman in his life whom Miriam did not like. Whatever the family thought, however, that was hardly a public crime.

She also knew that God had given words to her and felt she was being undermined. Maybe it was a reasonable feeling - but perhaps, too, she had forgotten that special relationship God had with Moses. It may also be that both she and some present-day writers overlooked the fact that when she had led that singing and dancing out of Egypt, she had only led the women! It would have been unseemly for it to have been otherwise – and sadly this has caused much heartache to modern women in those Christian denominations that adhere rigidly to the Old Testament models of leadership.

God, it seems, called her to account, was angry (?justifiably), and inflicted on her the worst of all punishments short of death - leprosy.

Despite her foolishness in letting her human nature intervene, the family bond remained strong and both brothers interceded for her healing, but to little avail. She was forced to spend the next seven days outside the camp, untouchable, despised, shamed, and she became one more delaying factor on the whole people's journey because no one was prepared to move on without her. As far as those outside her immediate family were concerned she remained loved and popular and attracted mass sympathy and support.

No more prophesying for Miriam. In one possibly jealous act she had blighted her life and ruined all prospect of ever seeing the

Promised Land. Her desire for power had robbed her of her influence. The prophetic gift had been taken away.

All human accolades are transitory. The lasting legacy of Miriam is encapsulated in the words of Jesus, 'Judge not ...'

Deborah ('the bee', 'the creature with the highest intelligence') was surely a pioneer among the women of her time - a prophetess and a judge in Israel.

She was married to Lapidoth, though we are told no more than his name. However, the very fact that his name is mentioned signified a position of his own in the community. It would be a very relevant fact to those who knew him. Deborah was to be found at her own particular pitch, under a palm named after her, between Ramah and Bethel, in Ephraim. She has been described as an agitator, one who was anxious for change and had the charisma to rouse people to action. Her position as one of the Judges made her a ruler, a leader - a unique individual at that time of female subordination.

The Israelites obviously respected her but did they altogether trust her? Perhaps that was why Barak was so determined to call her bluff, test her, see how far she could get without him. But she had pin-pointed him as the root of the trouble with their enemies, and told him straight that God had told him to go and meet Sisera, his response was in the region of, "No way, unless you go with me." He was the captain of Israel's armies, yet he was refusing to lead his men to Mount Tabor to confront their enemies.

Perhaps he thought she would refuse. Whoever, at that time in history, had heard of a woman going out to fight the battles in such blood-thirsty times? He could not have envisaged her becoming a militant heroine. Instead, far less fearful than he in the face of battle, she went, but it was to his detriment, for having once weakened and in essence begged a woman's support, whatever his reason for challenging her, he was now told that because of his cowardice, another woman would take the glory that should have been his.

A courageous woman and a cowardly man. What a combination for an encounter with the enemy. He even left it to her to name the day – and being a wise woman, she chose a day when the River Kishon was impassable to chariots as a great storm had caused serious flooding and made the valley into a sea of mud – and so Sisera's army was defeated. And it was Deborah, instead of Barak, who received great acclamation for the victory. She was immortalised in the victory songs of the people while his was a name to be forgotten.

But an even more courageous woman was waiting to deal with Sisera, the fleeing enemy general - **Jael**, the wife of Heber, a Kenite Bedouin, supposedly Sisera's ally. She was not a prophetess, nor even a member of one of the twelve tribes, but possibly for reasons of her own she was prepared to take matters into her own hands, regardless of the personal element of risk involved.

True to Deborah's prophecy, by the time Barak caught up with Sisera, intent on at least having the pleasure of disposing of him, Jael had already put an end to him - on the pretext of protecting him.

How should we regard a woman like Jael, dubbed 'The woman who killed a man while he slept'? As courageous, or treacherous? Certainly not courageous, says one because she dare not attack Sisera fairly. Enemy or not, she betrayed him, and for this she was to be for ever censured. Sadly, the Bible is full of such treachery, but on the 'right' side, it was always excused. She also violated the bounds of Hebrew hospitality.

However, Deborah had prophesied it, and now she and even Barak, possibly licking his wounds and trying to make the best of a bad situation, join in the victory song, though his glory is diminished by Jael's action. But instead of seeming to be aggrieved he sings about the situation, referring to 'the days of Jael' and the rise of Deborah 'as a mother in Israel'. And he could even join in a song that declared ...

> *Most blessed of women be Jael,*
> *the wife of Heber the Kenite,*
> *of tent-dwelling women most blessed.*

and went on with the gory details.

It leaves a mystery. All Jael had to do was to stand at the tent door and betray him, so why did she resort to the messy business of murder? Was it some sudden urge for recognition by Deborah, or was it a settlement of some old, unrecorded score? Or did she have another agenda? Names were prophecies in themselves and hers meant 'climber, always reaching for the heights', though that should not have gained her ends through treachery, rather by seizing the opportunity Sisera's arrival had given her to hand him over to his enemies.

But was it Deborah who added the other side - the anguish of the waiting mother, who, encouraged by her ladies, pictures Sisera victoriously dividing the booty and bringing her home a present? As not only a warrior but a poet, she could visualise with sensitivity the plight of the waiting women. Perhaps Lapidoth, too, had been a soldier. Unlike Miriam, she did not compromise her prophetic gifts but enhanced them.

And it was an unnamed woman who, years later, put an end to the traitor Abimelech, Gideon's son, by throwing a millstone at him from the top of the tower he was attacking, though he made his armour-bearer kill him so he wouldn't have the stigma of being killed by a woman! It seems that no matter how brave and courageous women were, they were still to be kept within bounds!

Another woman, **Huldah**, wife of Shallum, the keeper of the royal wardrobe, was a prophetess at the time of Josiah. Her role was to foretell the fall of Judah, though in Josiah's time peace was promised. She would hold court in the centre of the city and there people would visit her for counsel - almost, one might venture to say, as people would consult a fortune-teller today.

Her standing in Israel is marked by the fact that when Hilkiah found the book of the Law in the temple the king sent, not for Jeremiah but for Huldah, who had the unenviable task of forecasting the eventual destruction of Judah.

Nevertheless, it was a combination of her message and the public reading of the Law that fired King Josiah's reforms.

Interestingly, these women are all introduced in connection with a man – usually their husband, as it was he who gave them identity and standing in their community, though in Miriam's case it was her association with Moses and Aaron, her brothers and leaders of the Exodus from Egypt.

Married or not, the prophetesses were Advent Women in every sense of the word. They looked to the future with courage and conviction, unafraid to live out their prophecies to the last syllable.

THREE

Out of the shadows of patriarchal promises –
Three women, unique, filled with passion, hatred -
and love
in smaller doses.

Miriam the teenager –
    devious, opportunist
    not for herself alone
    but out of sister-love
    that stoops at nothing
    to achieve its end.
    Then she was strong.

Miriam, the prophetess –
    leading the dance of delight,
    unashamedly joyful,
    a bastion of hope
    for womankind.
    Her outraged passion has no bounds
    when death has stalked an enemy.

Miriam, the outcast –
    now grown old and jealous,
    misreading God,
    standing in judgment
    reaping consequence
    outside the camp –
    restored, to mourn her gift.

Deborah, the busy bee –
    not prophet only
    but judge among her people –
    a just and worthy judge,
    mother in Israel;
    decisions made with care,
    knowing God's good will.

Deborah, courageous to the core –
    unflinching in the face of war,
    prepared to over-rule
    the cowardice before,
    stand up, be counted,
    face the enemy
    as though alone.

And then came **Jael** –
    no prophet she, but schemer,
    stooping to gain a victory.
    Not meek and merciful
    but cruelly unkind,
    betraying trust,
    not caring who will mourn.

Jael, the temptress,
    strong against a friend turned foe.
    Only she could wield
    the instrument of power
    drive home the cruel nail of death;
    not in mortal combat, but in sleep,
    her courage lost in cowardice.

        Even the soldiers nailing Jesus to the cross
        would not have done so while he slept.

Three women – proud and passionate
in doing good
so dangerously.

9. CHALLENGING THE SYSTEM: THE DAUGHTERS OF ZELOPHEHAD AND ACHSAH

Numbers 27:1-11; 30:3-15; 36:1-12; Joshua 17:3-6
Joshua 15:13-19; Judges 1:11-15

Five women were bold enough to stand up for their rights - an activity that placed them far ahead of their time. These were **Mahlah, Noah, Hoglah, Milcah and Tirzah**, the daughters of Zelophehad, a descendant of Manasseh.

Their father had died in the wilderness wanderings, not through apostasy but nevertheless through his own fault. Because he had no male heirs his name could not be perpetuated. They challenged that ruling - why should their uncles have all his inheritance, leaving them with nothing, especially at such a crucial time when they were on the verge of entering the Promised Land? For if they were denied inheritance now, they would have no property rights there either, and as their father had possibly been quite well off, that was no small matter.

So, they took on the challenge of campaigning against male priority of inheritance – not for themselves only but for the many disinherited women who had asked the same question. They have been described as filing one of the earliest recorded lawsuits, one which still holds weight in a Court of Law.

They, however, sought an answer in the right direction – before God through their leader, Moses. A change was needed in the law, and they won their case, and not only their own but a ruling for all brotherless daughters thereafter - except for one clause introduced by their clan-conscious uncles: they must not marry outside the tribe so that the inheritance stayed within that family. Otherwise they lost it.

The wording surrounding this is ambiguous - 'Let them marry whom they think best' (i.e. no forced or arranged marriages), **only** it must be into a clan of their father's tribe that they are married.'

Some victory, we might think – appearing, as it does, incomplete and inconclusive. Yet its uniqueness lies in its assumption that in some circumstances some women could have some rights; and it is thus well ahead of the law at that time.

But did they do themselves and their successors any favours by capitulating? Was it tantamount to losing their case, especially when they even went so far as to marry their cousins, which ensured that their uncles still had some control of the inheritance? The important thing was that they had a **choice** and that was a tremendous step forward for their time. They had become human beings in the eyes of their society, and had they not considered their cousins acceptable husbands they still had the choice not to marry at all! There is just a hint of the 'Little Women' saga about this!

More seriously, there must have been an enormous amount of inbreeding among the tribes in such situations, and a resultant weakening of the strain. We may be thankful for the Book of Common Prayer's Table of Kindred and Affinity and see its purpose!

Yet it still wasn't a total victory for women as long as the only person not allowed to inherit was a wife, an injustice that was perpetuated for centuries.

Just a few verses, yet the outcome is momentous in the social history of the time. Women began to be noticed, to have individuality, even to be able to make vows - or pacts - with God. They helped make a difference in society, paving the way for so many other freedoms.

However, that could create problems since they were still regarded as 'owned' by their fathers or husbands. What happened if the man disapproved? Then she may be torn between loyalty to parent or spouse and that higher loyalty to God. It was a brave woman who would defy father or husband, however devoted a servant of God she was.

God Himself provides the solution: forgiveness. Forgiveness for having to forsake the vows.

This seems quaint in 21st century eyes, but then it was revolutionary. The fact that women were even permitted that covenant relationship was almost like our having 'the Vote' - something worth fighting for - at least then.

The rights of women were an emotive subject, legislated for even in wartime. Deuteronomy 21:10-14 outlines the procedure for marrying a woman captured in war; how she is not to be treated as a slave if the marriage doesn't work out. However, plain dislike is no ground for divorce and conditions were set out to protect women from this.

And rape was a crime punishable by death - of both parties if there was no sign that the woman sought help! The rules of sexual conduct and hygiene seem endless, but in those primitive conditions, how much disease did they help to avert?

It was not unusual for women to own territory, least of all while their husbands or fathers lived, but one woman, used as a ploy - or pawn - in war, decided to assert herself.

Achsah ('adorned') was Caleb's daughter so he put her up for gift to the one who could win Keriath-Sepher, the city of Debir, 'the City of the Book'. It was a carrot that could have drastically misfired for Achsah, but in the event, Othniel, her cousin, won her.

Whether she was consulted or not, she accepted her situation, but with an eye to business. Dubbed 'The Discontented Bride', first she requested Othniel to ask her father for a field as part of her dowry, probably knowing exactly which parcel of land Caleb would choose to part company with. And sure enough, he did just what she anticipated. Achsah has been severely criticised for what she did next because it seemed that whatever she had she wanted more. But was it so unreasonable to ask him for a present of the springs of water because she was in the Negeb, a desert region - and amazingly, he did - not one spring but two - upper and lower springs, referred to as Upper Gulloth and Lower Gulloth. Now they could make the land work for them, and ensure the stability of their relationship, for neither gift was worth anything worthwhile without the other! Othniel subsequently became one of Israel's judges.

Moving briefly beyond the Old Testament, it may be seen that Jesus acknowledged women as people with rights. In speaking of marriage Jesus saw the partnership as an equal one: ... *a man leaves his father and mother and gets married. He becomes like one person with his wife. Then they are no longer two people, but one.* An interesting thought, since it was common practice at the time for a man to divorce his wife on any pretext he chose. Jesus saw how loaded this was against the wife and forbade it unless she herself had deliberately committed adultery against her husband, and even then only at the last extreme. Thus he set women in a much better 'bargaining position' and gave them higher status as wives than ever before.

Women not only exerted their rights - they used their brains! Achsah has been seen as a tactful negotiator, yet with 'grace.' She possessed 'a divine discontent' – becoming, as it were, 'the mother of all aspiration and advancement.' Nevertheless, she remained respectful to her father, spoke reasonably, and pointed out the deficiency in the land he had made her dowry - it had no water! It wasn't necessarily easy, but she got double what she asked for - when the nether springs ran dry then the upper took over!

Again, Aschsah and Othniel won change, not for themselves only, but for all who followed.

It has been suggested that this incident forms a pattern of prayer, in which we do not ask for everything at once, like a child presenting its Christmas list, but employ patience and pray as need becomes apparent. First ask for the basic need (the field), then consider how it could work better, be more productive (add water), but pray modestly while using what has already been given – and then receive double what was asked for! This may, however, be an over-simplification of both Achsah's situation and a pattern of prayer!

Advent Women will think their requests through and define a pattern that is not unreasonable, and with grace and patience, and most of all, they will assert their right to the freedom of faith and worship that is becoming increasingly eroded.

JUDGMENT

God, You alone have the right to judge us,
whether we are right or wrong,
good or evil,
in Your will or out of it.

Only You can determine how we should act
and deal with our problems,
permitting no barriers
of who, what and where we are.

Only You have the power to call and delegate others
to work on Your behalf -
people who have themselves been judged
and not found wanting.

Lord God, so empower us
that we may be Your representatives,
people chosen to be Your advocates,
Your loyal servants in the world today.

10. COURAGE AND FORTITUDE: JEPHTHAH'S DAUGHTER

Judges 11:29-40

Some women are given a place in the Bible for just one act - sometimes bad, at others profoundly courageous. One such young lady isn't even named - Jephthah's daughter.

Why her name is not given is a mystery - or more likely an editorial oversight. She is both victim and martyr, abused and masochistic, wholly owned, yet self-giving.

Not the image of 21st century woman, unless she happens to live in an oppressed society. Jephthah's daughter certainly did.

Was her father hedging his bets or plain foolish, selfish or short-sighted when he pledged whoever came to greet him to God as a sacrifice if he won the battle against the Ammonites? It was all part of the superstition of the time, but for a religion that was not supposed to indulge in human sacrifice it was, even then, inexcusable. However, at that time the margins were still blurred and it is likely that Jephthah came from a pagan background where human sacrifice had been accepted as the norm.

It is one thing sacrificing material possessions - quite another making a burnt offering of your own daughter, especially when she is the only child and therefore truly a gift.

Unlike Abraham, there was no foreknowledge; no ram in the thicket; no going back.

She heard the sound of rejoicing and danced out to join the celebration, intent on pleasing him, only to find herself doing the opposite. Jephthah learnt the lesson of making over-hasty promises in that moment, of opening his mouth and putting his foot in it to maximum discomfort. He had secured the victory, yes - but he was far more of a loser than his opponent when this girl, full of life and promise, came into his view.

Was he, in that moment, hoping – praying even – that someone would come along and say, "But this is different: she's your daughter. God wouldn't want you to kill her"? But no one did. Instead, that brave girl, whose heart must have sunk to the pits, encouraged him to keep his promise.

Again, superstition - or dedication? Was she, in fact, the winner, the exemplar, the Christ-figure in the situation, willing to lay down her life for him rather than have him take it? The Psyche of the Old Testament.[10]

She brings a subtle twist into the action. No longer is she the subject of a vow. She is the wholly self-giving offering to God, worthy to be accepted by Him. Her attitude in effect takes away her father's guilt and responsibility for her death. (Has that the highest of all parallels in the self-giving of Jesus on the cross - the act that should have been seen to exonerate all those involved in putting him there of any particular guilt?)

Her example as a daughter is paramount. It is an act of forgiveness towards him for his own rashness. She understands sacrifice and service but sets a new boundary for it, one that brings to bear the fact that no one is entitled to take the life of another in God's Name.

Then she makes reparation for her father's guilt. Her sacrifice has to be self-sacrifice. He is now powerless against her.

Yet she was still his daughter and legally subject to him, so she actually asked permission to go and prepare herself, to come to terms with her own lost future - a husband, children, status in society, all precious, all to be cut off at a stroke.

He could have worried that she might not return, maybe even hoping she wouldn't, but he trusted her more than he trusted himself at that moment, and knew she was right. They both needed space to reflect on what they were doing.

But what actually was she doing in that time, and why did she make that request? Was it to prepare herself emotionally, mentally, spiritually perhaps? She had, putting it bluntly, received a death sentence. Had it been a sentence due to some fatal disease, such as cancer, she might have wanted to spend time with her friends, who would be equally distraught but lavish on her unconditional love.

Or did she, as some have suggested, latch on to the memory of their ancestor Abraham who was stopped from sacrificing his son at the last minute? Yet the way in which her father had presented her fate to her hardly suggested that **he** was being tested by God. On the contrary, he was the one who had attempted to test God. Perhaps it had never occurred to her that human sacrifice, for any reason, was anathema in Israel, so someone would eventually have to point that out and put a stop to it before Jephthah's sin compounded even more. Even with a pagan background, Jephthah should have known better than to promise to sacrifice any human being – and surely he should have thought it through enough to realise that the first to come rushing out to meet him wouldn't necessarily be the family dog!

Was his daughter even hoping to delay the inevitable, or that some other solution might be found? Or was she spending her time in prayer, offering all the things she might have been to God, every experience that would now never be hers. Or did she simply want to get away from her parents – and with a father like that, who wouldn't? We are not told the reaction of her mother but it's not difficult to imagine.

In the light of Israel's attitude to human sacrifice, however, there is a theory, based on the cultural norms of the time, that instead of being a human sacrifice, Jephthah's daughter was to be sacrificed to the service of the Tabernacle, losing her freedom and spending the rest of her life there, cut off from family and friends. That would explain why she wanted to go away – simply to spend some time with her friends and have a little enjoyment before the crunch moment came. Death in those circumstances might even have been preferable!

An alternative view sees the result of that vow as a punishment to Jephthah for making it and whether or not the sentence amounted to death, surely this is right, for no one, not even a father, should have such power to wield over another person's life - even had the person who stepped over his threshold been the least of his slaves.

Scholars are divided on their interpretation of events, but two things do stand out. For many years thereafter the Israelites honoured Jephthah's daughter with a four-day festival each year, not so much to lament over her, as well they might, but to celebrate her courage and commitment. The second thing is less understandable. In the list of the faithful in Hebrews 11 is the name of Jephthah. This can only be because he made a vow to God and kept it, regardless of cost - but surely, while the cost to him was high, the cost to his daughter went through the roof. Therefore, it is she not he whose name should be included in that list.

She, not he, is the faithful and righteous one, and it is a great pity that we have no name for her. Today she would have been hailed a saint and martyr.

Advent Women are the stuff that saints and martyrs are made of - utterly selfless, courageous, committed, frequently persecuted and often left in obscurity.

📖 📖 📖 📖 📖

PROMISES

Lord, save us from the sin of Jephthah,
making rash promises we cannot – should not – keep,
the kind of vows that come unthinking from our lips
and cannot be rescinded.

Lord, help us to realise
that you want **our** lives, freely given not to death but life,
lived in all its fullness in your Name
and for your sake.

Help us to learn to let go selfish interests,
do nothing that will do another harm,
make only promises that we can keep
to do another good and glorify your Name.

Help us to be the one with courage and commitment,
facing what life throws out, accepting, taking all to you,
committed to her promises to serve you steadfastly,
sacrificing self to salve another's guilt –

the way you did by going to the cross.

11. MOTHERS IN ISRAEL

**Judges 13:2-24; 14:1-20; 17:1-18:26; 1 Samuel 1-2:21;
2 Kings 18:1-8**

Barrenness and birth are key issues in the Old Testament, for to be childless was counted as deficient in womanhood. Time and again we find women pleading for a child - Sarah, Rebekah, Rachel, and now this unnamed **wife of Manoah**.

Despite the fact that this birth story is told to lay the foundation of Samson's lifestyle, it nevertheless seems remiss that there is no mention of his mother's name. It is as though she didn't matter, was just a means to an end in the writer's scheme of things. Yet that is not how the narrative reads. However, according to the Talmud, her name was **Hazzelelponi** (mentioned in I Chronicles 4:3 as daughter of Etam, a descendant of Hur), or **Zeleponi**, which means 'the shadow falls over me'. She certainly lived in the shadow of her husband, but also under the shadow of God's concern. Deeply disappointed she may have been, but she was also privileged to receive a revelation from God, who recognised her piety and so made her happy for a season, though she was to be given much sorrow by the son she had so desired.

Here, in fact, was a woman who listened and was far more spiritually aware than her husband. When the angel appeared she immediately recognised that here was a man of God, even though he told her nothing about himself. Manoah, on the other hand, was a doubting Thomas. "Unless I see for myself ..."

But the man still visited the woman first, and she had to rush off and find her husband, who was full of doubts and questions ...

"Who are you?"

"Why won't you eat?"

And then, when he had been persuaded to offer thanks to God, he saw the man for the angel he was, and was terrified, sure they would die because they had 'seen God'! But would a God who intended to kill them have accepted their offering? And would He have made such wonderful promises in vain? Of course not. Manoah deserved his level-headed wife's contempt.

This unnamed woman had an accepting faith, an inherent instinct that recognised God's presence in their lives.

Here was an Advent Woman who could walk forward in confidence and trust, sure of God's presence and protection. And a woman who took to heart all that the angel had said and denied herself for the sake of her unborn child. A true mother in Israel.

But what exactly had she to commit her child to? One who had taken a Nazirite vow (or had one made on their behalf) was consecrated to God and pledged never to cut his hair, drink wine or touch a corpse during the period of the vow – which could be for a limited period or, in the case of the one made on behalf of Samson, for life.

Unfortunately, such mothers don't always have an easy life. Rebekah was plagued by Esau's choice of foreign wives. Just so, when Samson, who seemed so wise and Godly and was dedicated to the Nazirite way of life, decided he wanted a Philistine wife, how perturbed his parents were.

"She pleases me. Get her for me."

A demand they found so difficult to answer, but they were unable to stand in his way. They also didn't know how strong their son had become - or where his supply of honey came from! How did they feel when the marriage seemed to last only a week and he wrought such havoc in Ashkelon?

But what about **Micah's Mother** and her muddled theology? First she curses the one who stole her money. When Micah returns it with full confession, then she declares he will be blessed by the Lord. Having said that, she then turns two hundred pieces of that silver into an idol, which she gives him - a pagan symbol.

So he makes a shrine to this god and even makes his own son a priest, so that instead of drawing closer to the One God he moves farther away.

But his mother had believed in a blessing!

Eventually, having had his idol stolen, along comes a Levite to bring that blessing and turn the tide of his life back to God.

Advent Woman? Or a woman herself seeking an Advent promise for her son? And then seeing it fulfilled in spite of herself!

Perhaps they both had to learn to live without their idolatrous props: the Bible does not tell us what happened to them after the Danites stole the idol - or what happened to the Danites!

Samson's mother was to lose her son to the Lord, Micah's mother ran the risk of losing him from the Lord.

A third mother, the most well-known, is **Hannah**. Like Rachel before her, Hannah had a rival, Peninnah, who had children while Hannah had none, though Elkanah, her husband, made the mistake of Jacob in regarding her as favourite and loving her most. Not surprisingly, Peninnah flaunted herself in front of Hannah.

Hannah was so unhappy it made her ill and she cried bitterly to God when they went to the temple, so much so that Eli mistook her for a drunk!

As a last resort, Hannah begged for a son and to her lips came a new word as she knelt in distress in the temple: **IF** ... a little word with a big meaning and a lot of undercurrents. Like Gideon before her she laid out her fleece, but this time it wasn't a fleece to convince herself, but to bait God, to try in one last, desperate attempt to get an answer to her prayer. "If you will give me a son I will give him back to You."

On the other hand, did this denote the moment of change in her? The moment when, in her own way, she said, 'Not mine but Thine'? She wanted a son, needed to bear a son, needed the satisfaction of proving herself to her husband and his other wife, and to the neighbourhood in general, of knowing that she was capable of fulfilling all the instincts of motherhood. Her mistake, however, was that she wanted him for herself. In her desperation she suddenly realised that if God gave her the miracle she so desired then she owed something back to Him. And it must be nothing short of the very gift that she herself desired.

So she promised she would give him back to God. Like Manoah's son he would become a Nazirite from birth.

Once he realised she was in earnest Eli gave her his blessing and told her to "Go in peace." At this she cheered up, and returned home full of faith that all would work out, which of course it did.

It does seem rather rough on Elkanah to have the son of his most-loved wife taken from him and offered permanently to God, but he had to let her do it because he recognised what having the child had meant to her and that God had answered a deeply felt prayer. And after all, it was hardly the kind of rash vow Jephthah had made. Hannah was not promising in blind faith but with her eyes wide open to reality. Wherever he was, her child would live and grow to manhood.

Now it was time to put Eli in his place and quash his misunderstanding once for all. But her phraseology is odd: "I have **lent** him to the Lord" - and contradictory: "he is **given** to the Lord."

But what kind of mother can leave a two-year-old with an old man? Answer: one who is wholly dedicated to God and keeps her promises to Him. Yes, but couldn't she have waited a little longer, till the child had begun to gain a little independence, start his education?

On the other hand, it wasn't as though he was lost to her for ever. Every year she would go back to the temple and take him a new robe, so she was able to see her first-born son at each stage of his life. She was also blessed with five other children, three sons and two daughters.

It is significant that in these instances of blessing the barren, while the son is clearly the most important, God never ignores the daughters. They, too, are part of His blessing, His bounty.

How does Hannah react to this? Does she see her unexpected family as a reward, or a bonus? And her daughters? Helpers in her old age? People who will care for her if her husband dies first?

Finally there is **Abi**, or Abijah, a lesser known woman, not one who found herself unable to have children, but named because she was a member of the royal household in Israel. One reason her name was mentioned may have been the significance of it - 'My Father is Jehovah' or 'The Will of God.' Israelites believed in names. They placed all their hopes for their children into their names and somehow they were expected to live up to those expectations.

This raises a question: was it indeed the will of God that she became a queen? The answer may lie in the nature of the three men around whom her life revolved. Firstly, Zechariah, her father. We know very little about him and there are no less than thirty men of that name in the Bible, but he was obviously a Godly man and one who understood visions of God and had even had some contact with Isaiah. But what were his hopes for his daughter? Did he believe God had some purpose for her, or was it a sigh of resignation at having a daughter in a country where sons were so coveted?

The second man, her husband Ahaz, was her extreme opposite - Godless and hard, the kind of man no committed Christian would freely choose to marry. He was a man who put politics before principles; he preferred intrigue with the enemy to the sound, spiritual advice of Isaiah. He left his country virtually destitute, not only financially but morally, for he was a dabbler in idolatrous cults, not only worshipping a pagan god, but experimenting in 'lewd and violent' activities. Abi's role as queen to this man must have been hard to cope with.

It is through the third man, her son Hezekiah, that we learn most about her. In great faith she had named him 'Strong in the Lord' and brought up in such a strongly divided household, he had chosen to follow the example of his mother, turning away from idols and seeking inspiration from God. He was not afraid to stand up to the King of Assyria in whose hands, thanks to Ahaz, they had been slaves. He set his people on their feet again, bringing them back to God.

So Abi's witness must have been a glowing one, unafraid to profess her Lord despite adversity. As the queen in Israel she was in a unique position of influence, and though she had no effect on Ahaz, undaunted, she overcame the opposition and led her son in the right path, teaching him about God and the way He had led and helped Israel in the past. The result was that Hezekiah instigated a great national religious revival, and put the Name of Yahweh back on everyone's lips. Thus it could not be disputed that it was the will of God that she should be the queen of Israel.

*Advent Women find no difficulty in identifying the course God's plan will take and living with it. They pray - they trust - they offer thanks and gifts - and then travel on, assured in their hearts that God **will** be with them.*

THANKSGIVING

God, who answers prayer,
even the jumbled prayer of desperation
from one who cannot be a mother,
the barren life, betrayed by circumstance,
You heard - even as the priest did not
who thought that I was drunk.
Well, now I bring him wine and sacrifice -
a double sacrifice, a treble gift:
the handsome bull - he could have
bought us much at market price -
new clothes, more furniture, warm blankets
for the child -
but now the child is here, and here he stays,
not given - I cannot forfeit every right
to one so precious, cannot withhold my mother love -
so I will lend him to You, God,
and visit every year with gifts
and let him know my gratitude,
and that I love him still.

12. RUTH AND NAOMI: STRANGERS AND SOJOURNERS

The Book of Ruth

The story of **Ruth** is that of Advent Woman Supreme - yet alone her story simply could not have happened. She needed the two other female players in her drama to consolidate the action. Firstly, there was **Naomi**, the woman who became a sojourner in Moab through the will of her husband; then **Orpah**, her sister-in-law, with whom she shared the common bonds, not only of sisterhood but of widowhood. Orpah was her natural soulmate, the non-stranger who in some unforeseen way became a stranger.

We need to consider the background in order fully to understand this story - a story which opens in Moab, a foreign land as far as the people of Judah were concerned, even though it was little more than thirty miles away, on the other side of the Dead Sea. That they had shared heritage through Abraham was something the Judeans preferred to forget! One of the Judeans, Elimelech, had married Naomi and they had two sons, Mahlon and Chilion, everything a Hebrew family could wish for - that is, until famine struck.

That famine has been taken by some as a sign that God was displeased with His people because they had turned away from Him and someone as highborn as Elimelech should have been at the forefront of the movement back to true religion. Instead, hearing that there was food in Moab, Elimelech uprooted his family from their home in Bethlehem and travelled to that foreign land, where they lived for some time; so long, in fact, that the sons grew to marriageable age while they were there.

It has actually been suggested that the real reason behind the move was the health of these two sons, that they were weak, sickly children who couldn't have survived a famine.

It would have been usual for a devout Jew to think of returning home to seek wives for his sons, or at the very least sending to some past neighbours who might have eligible daughters, as Abraham had done, but Elimelech didn't do either of these things. In fact, it rather seems that he died before taking action of any kind. Consequently, it appears that the sons did their own thing and chose wives from the Moabites, probably girls they'd grown up with. However, this may not have been the selfish act some critics would like us to think, and subsequent events certainly give no substance to that argument. After all, a precedent had already been set in the family and Naomi at least would know about that. And it would seem that they found their wives from good families; some have suggested that they may well have been from Lot's direct descendants, though that was hardly any cause for pride.

Then further disaster struck. Not only was Elimelech dead but now, ten years on, his sons also died. We are not told how, since all three must have been men in their prime. One suggestion is that it could have been a form of malaria virulent in that country; another puts it down to extravagant living. Somewhere there may just be the vaguest hint of retribution for Elimelech's act of betrayal, 'stepping outside the will of God', ignoring the warnings, travelling from Bethlehem, 'the house of bread' to Moab, plain 'nothingness.' It certainly substantiates the belief that widowhood was some kind of curse or punishment.

However it may be seen, the story opens with the plight of three widows, left to fend for themselves in what is to one a foreign land, and to the others a land they have forsaken by choice. For a time they were as one, both intent on staying with their mother-in-law, whether out of pity or love, or a common bond of widowhood, it is hard to say. But Naomi faced them with hard facts: there was little hope of a future with her, even with her own family since the gulf of time and circumstance had been immense; they would be entering what, to them, would be foreign territory. Perhaps they might suffer rejection.

On the other hand, did Naomi contemplate their family situation? She herself felt she was returning ashamed and empty, so how would two young women fare among their own family, doing the same thing? Perhaps not. Those two women had become Naomi's property, all she had left in the way of inheritance from her deceased sons. It is really her story. She, as far as women were able in those chauvinistic days, was the real owner of the land forfeited by her late husband; she was the one desperate for a future, in need of friends, in need of a positive rather than a negative identity, of a sense of place, of respect and a position in society made possible only by kindred and heirs. Ruth became the mere appendage by whom all these things came her way – she could almost be called a pawn.

Both were Moabites, born and bred. They were given the natural choice of returning home to their own families, whatever their reception was likely to be, or to commit themselves to Naomi – to choose freedom or, in effect, chains. In the event, either Orpah risked it and Ruth couldn't face it, **or** Orpah couldn't face the unknown while Ruth rose to the challenge.

Clearly both held Naomi in high regard or the situation would never have arisen - they would automatically have returned home. To suggest otherwise, of Orpah in particular, is to do her an injustice. But she was not Advent Woman. She dare not branch out alone, even with other women. She needed a man, even if that man were only to be her father. In her case, a mother-in-law was no substitute.

Ruth saw things differently. But was it that she saw herself as being dismissed and couldn't cope with it, or that some spiritual instinct rose in her and made her dare to abandon the known for the unknown, to take on board this foreign mother, her family, her country and, most importantly, her God - and the statement she made has been passed down the centuries as an example of utter commitment to the service of the Living God. But it was a blind commitment in every sense of the word, and God was holding her to it.

From Naomi's point of view the girl was company, and she very soon realised that she could be of use to her as well. They arrived at harvest time, and Ruth didn't need much prompting to see that there was a way in which she could ensure that neither of them starved, demeaning as the work of gleaning might be. A proud woman could not even have thought of it. Ruth was made of stern stuff!

And it must have been pretty nerve-wracking for her, a total stranger, to tag on behind the local regulars, those who worked day in, day out to bring in a meagre living.

Had she known she was the subject of close scrutiny, it might have been worse still, but Boaz, whether because he was smitten with her or because he recognised Naomi as family fallen on hard times, invited her to stay in his fields and on the side ensured there was plenty for her to glean.

A number of things have been pointed out here, one being the fact that however Boaz felt about Naomi and Ruth, there was no automatic hand-out. She was given the means and opportunity to work for it - and under fair conditions of employment, which included adequate meal breaks.

Was she so innocent that she didn't ask why? Or Suspect? Boaz had his answer - her own selfless treatment of and commitment to Naomi.

What made Ruth even more special was that she was the innocent one, not the opportunist. That role fell to Naomi when she suddenly realised the implication of Boaz's interest: the rights of a next of kin.

But who was Naomi really interested in when she spoke of securing the future? Ruth's, or her own? And did she, in fact, take advantage of Ruth's ignorance of Jewish customs?

Innocent Ruth was the model of obedience - but she was abused and exploited, though not by Boaz. As Naomi put her daughter-in-law at risk, even so Boaz protected her from any hint of immorality or misjudgment, for had people known what was going on, Ruth would have found her shame far in excess of anything widowhood had brought her.

The Book of Ruth gets away with murder because generally people don't understand the implications of Levirite marriage. Naomi was exposing her daughter-in-law to the most incredible risks. Using her in order to compromise Boaz could have cost Ruth, at best her reputation, at worst her life. Happily for all of them, it was her complete, if blind, following of the rules that led her to that new husband Naomi couldn't give her.

There is no question that Boaz realised very early on what Naomi was plotting but played along with it because he had found in Ruth's own innocence and dedication to her mother-in-law a very special quality which made her attractive to him. Naomi herself does not come out of this narrative at all well, but needs to be understood in context. Poverty coupled with pride drove her to exploit Ruth. It is little wonder, therefore, that the Bible emphasises that Boaz was just and fair, and that his liking for Ruth ensured that he also respected her. The account leaves readers in no doubt that God had a very fatherly eye on the situation and that was why it turned out as it did.

Nevertheless, the manner in which it was done leaves us with 21st century questions – "I have acquired ... all that belonged to Elimelech ... and Chilion and Mahlon ... and also Ruth the Moabite ..."

His intentions may have been totally honourable, but 'acquiring' a wife, even one who appeals, is hardly the same as buying cattle or sheep! Again, we have to see it in the context of a legally binding agreement of the time.

Of course, Ruth could have refused to agree to Naomi's scheme, but it seems that Ruth loved Naomi enough to take the risk of obedience. She made a choice, albeit it was not totally an informed choice, possibly made under duress because of Naomi's plight. In the end, both were rewarded, and her name and nature have had far-reaching effects on Christian history, the only one greater being

Mary, the Mother of Jesus, whose obedience was without precedent.

Advent Women are not only bold and venturesome and totally committed. They know how to love. It is a natural instinct.

LOYALTY

What bitterness!
The old woman, worn by grief, empty,
yet full of her own misfortune.

Your God - my God!
How soon she had forgotten,
failed the God Who'd given her the gift -
one life to win for Him.

Your people - my people.
How would anyone accept a God
of such misfortune! How could she overlook
the riches of humanity set free?

Where you go, I go.
She had a choice - the old familiar land,
or to become a sojourner,
ripe for injustice, rights denied?

She chose her course
and set her destiny.

+++

Lord, may we be constant in love,
loyal in service,
and trusting to the end.

13. DYNASTY

1 Samuel 14:49-50a; 18:17-29; 19:11-17; 25:2-43
2 Samuel 2:1-4; 3:2-16; 5:13-16; 6:12-16, 20-23; 11:2-12:24;
13:1-39; 21:1-14
1 Kings 1:1-53; 2:13-25; 3:1; 7:8b; 9:15-17,24; 11:1-40

With the first king of Israel, from 1020 BC, there began a dynasty that rose and fell as loyalty ebbed and flowed, and just occasionally, as though an after-thought, the chroniclers seemed to remember that no such dynasty can exist without its women, and then, unusually, they name them, e.g.

Saul's wife - **Ahinoam** (daughter of Ahimaz)
and his daughters - **Merab and Michal**

Merab should have become David's wife because of his success and an unfulfilled promise - but instead she was given to Adriel the Mehdathite.

Why? Because David had felt himself unworthy of the king's daughter, but when Saul discovered that his youngest, Michal, actually loved David, he decided she would be a good way to entrap him, as he was jealous of David's success. However, his ploy didn't work because David fulfilled the bride price set and Michal won the man she loved - at least for the time being.

But whose side was she on when it mattered? Like her brother, Jonathan, she initially protected him and warned him of danger, helping him to escape - a brave act against her own father.

Sadly, if there was ever a snare for David it was women. **Abigail** was the next to attract his attention, a woman 'clever and beautiful,' married to a mean, surly husband, Nabal - so mean that he courted disaster when he refused to give sustenance to David's army.

Fortunately, when Abigail heard of it she took the matter into her own hands, and her quick-thinking smoothed the matter over and averted a bloodbath. She was, as David said, a woman of 'good sense' - so much so that when Nabal's own guilt and debauchery resulted in his death, David claimed her as his wife.

But for David even she wasn't enough and he added **Ahinoam** of Jezreel to his harem (by which time Saul had taken Michal back and given her to someone else, as though she were a piece of furniture being reclaimed by the bailiffs).

David also had other wives ...

Maacah, daughter of Talmai of Geshur
Haggith - **Abital** – **Eglah**

Since only Ahinoam and Abigail are mentioned as travellers with him, these others must have been acquired after his accession, no doubt to help guarantee the succession. That in itself was to prove disastrous, as it resulted in his becoming father to six sons by six different wives ...

Amnon   (Ahinoam)
Chileab (Abigail)
Absalom (Maacah)
Adonijah   (Haggith)
Shephatiah (Abital)
Ithream (Eglah)

All of them were born in Hebron.

And there was another woman in the picture – **Rizpah** (to whom we shall return), not one of David's wives, but Saul's concubine, whom Abner, Saul's army captain, had appropriated for himself. That liaison, right as Ishbaal (Saul's son) was to question it, was to cost Saul's line their dynasty, for Abner turned on Ishbaal and sold them to their enemies.

But even that had conditions. David, with six wives, wanted Michal back - dragged from her distraught husband by Saul's captain. Michal, however, despised him for his impropriety and showiness. To her he was not a man worthy of respect. She spoke her mind and her heart as a wife, more caring about his reputation as a man than as a king - a man she knew to be attractive to women. But she paid the price by being denied motherhood, which debased her honour and perhaps helped to turn her towards idolatry.

Sadly, she would despise his actions even more by the time she died. All the victories in the world did him no honour before his wife - and maybe not any of them. Today we might see him in the guise of a ruthless guerrilla leader, and but for the women in his life and ancestry, he might not have become the man he did. He had even made his sons priests.

Once he had Jerusalem David took more wives and had eleven more sons. How typical that, honour apart, the one who had many should desire one more - and that was the day he looked out and saw **Bathsheba** bathing.

David may have been gentle over the shedding of some blood, such as Abner's, but he was not innocent when it came to Uriah, his loyal captain, killed because of his own innocent loyalty and David's adultery.

The story of David and Bathsheba, who seemed to play more of a passive role than either Michal or Abigail, is one of God's forgiveness. Bathsheba herself was not afforded much choice but was literally taken by the desire of the king of Israel. Could she have refused, other than at peril of her life? As it was, she had much to learn. Her beauty obviously made her a trifle vain, and it could be that she was bored and disenchanted with her husband. The reference to her in Matthew's genealogy is almost a grudging one, for it seems he cannot even bear to call her by her own name; in his eyes she was and always would be Uriah's wife. Yet the doubts in this do not rest with Bathsheba, but against David who became the great forerunner of the Messiah in spite of them. The child of their illicit union died, but the next child, Solomon, lived and was loved and elevated way above his brothers.

What kind of parental example does that make God when the Bible blatantly tells us, 'The Lord loved him.' The child of consolation. The child who, by rights, should never have been born!

But the prophet had predicted trouble in the royal household, and with so many half-brothers and wives that was not surprising - nor was the fact that Amnon, the eldest, Ahinoam's son, fell in love with his step-sister **Tamar**, daughter of Maacah. Add a ruthless, deceitful friend and there is a recipe for disaster.

Tamar was used and abused. She had obeyed her father and trusted Amnon, believing his story - and she tried to reason with him, for both their sakes - but he raped her and then he despised her because he'd had his own way. There had been no love, only lust. And after all that she was even abused in a different way by her own brother, who tried to keep Amnon's act quiet, for all his hatred of him. Sadly, David, who was keen to punish outsiders, would not punish Amnon, his eldest and (at the time) best-loved son.

Tamar, one innocent woman, became the centre of the prophetic declaration and there was no peace in the family from that day. Absalom killed for her, fled because of her, and then named his own daughter after her.

Yet Tamar was not the only abused woman. Saul's concubine, **Rizpah**, had two sons, Armoni and Mephibosheth and Saul's daughter, **Merab**, wife of Adriel, had five sons, all of whom were handed over to the Gibeonites as recompense for Saul's treatment of them, to be hung up on the trees. And Rizpah mourned and stood guard all through the harvest till her sons and the others had been given a decent burial with Saul and Jonathan rather than be eaten by the vultures. Of all the women in those bloody days, Rizpah was the one who stood out as a mother. Her devotion has been described as unmatched in literature. Maacah stayed in the shadows, apparently accepting her daughter's fate and distancing herself from Absalom's revenge. Merab had already died and it was Michal who had brought up her children.

But Rizpah's act was no brief protest. She stayed with those decomposing corpses for months, determined that they would not be disgraced in death as they had been in the manner of their death. It had meant sleepless nights, agonising days, and in the heat of the sun a totally sickening environment. She risked her own life to keep this vigil but the Gibeonites had had their revenge and left her alone. Only when King David heard what she was doing did he send and have the bodies taken down and buried with Saul and Jonathan - father and step-brother - all equal in death as they had been unequal in life. And Rizpah was able to go home and resume her life, her less edifying activities now completely obliterated by her maternal nobility.

The last of David's women was **Abishag**, a beautiful Shunammite pressed into service to tend to the ageing king's needs, though not as a wife.

But when David died that was not the last to be heard of Abishag. For some inexplicable reason Adonijah decided he wanted her as his wife, but the request cost him his life. Solomon had decided it was a plot. Bathsheba, as Solomon's mother, was involved in the plotting of Nathan and others to ensure that Adonijah did not become king on his father's death (as technically, being the third son and oldest survivor, he should have done).

But **did** David promise his throne to Solomon, the **youngest** son? Was that why Adonijah did not invite Solomon along with other brothers to his sacrifice?

Perhaps Bathsheba would have sought her son's rights without prompting from Nathan; as a mother that would have been instinctive – just as the mother of James and John, 'the sons of thunder', tried to wangle preference with Jesus for her sons.

Then again, as a prophet should Nathan have worked so surreptitiously? Was it out of pique - or suspicion - because he and Zadok, Benaniah and Solomon himself had been left out of the invitations? Using Bathsheba wasn't bound to win his case, but it worked!

Solomon himself married Pharaoh's daughter - a **foreigner** - and built her a palace, but she isn't even named. However, she was the subject of 'an alliance' ... 'taken ...' and she had come with quite a dowry - the city of Gezer which he had destroyed.

And added to Pharaoh's daughter were seven hundred princesses and three hundred concubines, for women were his weakness, too, and his downfall. Just one wife was named - **Naamah**, an Ammonite, the mother of Rehoboam, the son who would initially succeed him.

Many of the mothers of Israel's kings are named, one being **Maacah**, Abishalom's daughter and mother of Abijam, Rehoboam's son. But Maacah is also named as Abijah's son Asa's mother! She suffered the fate of being deposed as Queen Mother by her own son because she had made an image of the pagan goddess Asherah.

And there were those in Israel itself who became Solomon's enemies - one being the son of another named woman, **Zeruah**, a widow, wife of Nebat, the mother of Jeroboam who was to be Solomon's future successor in Israel.

History has often shown that a mother figure will be at the head of a vast dynasty – we only have to see how far and wide the influence of Queen Victoria spread through her children, and more recently, there has been Rose Kennedy in America.

Many other mothers are mentioned in the annals of the kings of Israel and Judah, indicating that whatever the status of women, these held an abiding influence over their royal sons.

Advent is a season when the world's attention becomes focused on motherhood - and one mother in particular - whose son was to become Messiah, the longed-for successor to King David.

EDITING

Crime – and punishment!
How does it square with a God of Love
who may exact repentance but forgives, not punishes?
What vicious editing ascribes to God such vengeance –
too much to bear the text, or consequence?
Fear and disobedience
mingle with the blessing of the innocent,
jealousy, resentment, judged embarrassment turn on enmity
and life-long comments of disdain
without posterity.
Hatred cannot love,
it breeds contempt
and barrenness.

14. THE BRAVE ONES

2 Samuel 17:15-22; 15:13-16; 20:3-22; 1 Kings 3:16-28;
10:1-13; 14:1-18; 17
2 Kings 4:1-37; 5:1-14
Joshua 2:1-24; 6:17, 22-25
The Book of Esther

In 1948 Norah Lofts wrote that for her 'dynamite is a harmless substance, lightly to be handled' compared with the Old Testament![11] Maybe that thought is at its most cogent during those times recorded in the Bible when women take the initiative and couple deceit with bravery. Such was the **wife of a well-owner at Bahurim** who hid Ahimaaz and Jonathan, David's emissaries, from Absalom's pursuing servants - but to do so successfully she had to lie and send them in the wrong direction.

Then there was the **wise woman** who dared to summon Joab, David's bloodthirsty captain, to go to listen to her. She had the peace of Israel at heart and wanted to dissuade him from destroying the whole city. But to achieve her aim, she had to persuade her fellow-countrymen to give up Sheba, a traitor, for the sake of them all. Did that set a precedent for that ultimate sacrifice of one man for the sake of the whole community we read of in the Gospels?

Joab could have back-tracked on his word, or thought it a trap and had her killed, but instead, he **listened**.

But what about those **ten wives** (possibly concubines) David left to mind his house at Jerusalem? What had they done to merit being locked up under guard as though in prison? Had he not wanted them any more shouldn't they have been set free? Or did he have a legal obligation? They were treated like widows, in shame.

Then there was another self-sacrificing act, when **two mothers** gave birth to babies and one was accidentally suffocated. For two prostitutes to find themselves arguing in front of a king seems bizarre. Even more bizarre was the wise king's verdict - one live child, one dead one, so, cut the live one in half!

One mother immediately agreed, but the other was cut to the heart. "No! Give him to her - let him live not die!"

And the king could have done just that. It was a risk, but one that only a real caring mother would challenge - so her child was restored to her. The incident is recorded to demonstrate Solomon's wisdom, but perhaps it tells us far more about the quality of motherhood.

But could any good mothers make a pact to kill and eat their babies at a time of famine? Surely a good mother would have starved herself first rather than take the life of her innocent child. The deceptive mother who hid her child was no more commendable. The proposal to make a pact was no less a sin than putting it into practice. Yet what their desperate actions did do was initiate the end to the conflict that had brought the people to their knees in the first place.

The Bible contains stories of bad women as well as good ones – and there are many more than the familiar names of Jezebel and Delilah! For example, did Asa's God-fearing wife **Azubah** have no influence over Jehoshaphat, who turned out to be as wicked as his father, Asa? Did that make her guilty of failing in his education? And was the fact that Jehoram's wife was Ahab's daughter the reason he turned away from the Lord?

And there was **Athaliah**, the mother of Ahaziah (Jehoram's son). His relationship to Ahab made him go wrong, so when Ahaziah died, Athaliah reacted by killing the whole of the royal family – or so she thought! But she had reckoned without Ahaziah's sister, **Jehosheba**, who smuggled his baby son Joash and his nurse away into the temple and saved them. That was a very brave act because it could have cost her her own life. Thinking she was safe and in total control, Athaliah reigned as Queen in Judah for six years - till Joash was seven years old. Joash's own mother, **Zibiah** from Beersheba had obviously been an influence for good, for Joash was a man of peace, though he died as a result of a conspiracy.

Another woman who presented herself to Solomon was the **Queen of Sheba**. She was to Solomon as Thomas was to Jesus - a doubter who needed convincing, a woman who dared to ask questions but who had the courage to know when she was beaten. An honest doubter.

Jeroboam's wife was sent by her cowardly husband to seek help from the prophet Ahijah when Abijah, their son, became sick. She went in disguise, but the prophet was forewarned. It was a brave woman who took Ahijah's dire prophecy back to her husband, knowing that her son would die the moment her feet crossed the threshold.

But how brave was she? Would she have been braver to have been more God-fearing and to have refused her husband's request? There were, after all, limits to a wife's obedience, even then.

Bravery was not in the deceit but in the outcome. With the burden of Ahijah's prophecy weighing her down she could have turned away and not gone home, leaving her husband to work it out for himself. Had she thought it through rationally, she might even have said, "If I don't go home he won't die." She was brave in that she was prepared to face the truth, knowing how she was implicated, and knowing what it meant for both her husband and her son.

Advent Women don't flinch from the truth, however much they may have strayed from it and however much, in the end, it might hurt them.

The **Widow of Zarephath** was not afraid to challenge Elijah when she felt let down, though she had been quick to exercise faith in God and obey him when he turned up on her doorstep demanding a meal at a time when she had nothing to spare during a serious drought. He promised then that she would never be short of meal or oil during the crisis, and everything was fine for the family until one day her son took ill and died. Then she blamed Elijah as though, having saved them from starvation, he had been responsible for the onset of illness. It was a natural reaction, but can't have gone down very well with Elijah. However, instead of making matters worse by reacting against her accusations, he said nothing but took the boy to his room laid him down, prayed to God in an accusatory manner, and then, in effect, gave him the kiss of life and resuscitated him.

And the result of that incident was the admission by the Widow that even with the continuous supply of food she had doubted his credentials, but now she had been totally convinced.

We might ask whether she was right to have doubts that Elijah was who he said he was – just as we today need to question every doorstep salesmen, or offers that look too good to be true. She could so easily have been taken in, had her obvious vulnerability exploited.

But **Widows** were often made the subject of miracles. The widow of one of the prophets, deeply in debt and unable to feed her two sons, was in dire straits - until she approached Elisha who ensured that her jar of oil produced and produced until she was able to raise enough to pay her debts and live.

Sometimes, however, the women were neither poor nor widows. **The Shunammite Woman** who gave Elisha food and a bed had means, intuition and common sense, and she could see where need lay. She was rewarded by the gift of a son, only to have him die. But hers was a vigorous faith, even though she was unafraid to face Elisha with her anger, refusing to return home without him, which in turn led to another miracle of resuscitation. Later he also warned her of impending famine.

But who was she? Rabbinic tradition has identified her with Abishag of Shunem, the young girl brought in to companion David in his dying days, but there does not seem to be much support for this since few commentaries on the account actually name her.

She has been called the Great Woman of Shunem – with emphasis on the **Great** rather than where she came from. Shunem was situated between Mount Carmel, Elisha's home, and Jezreel, the Israelite capital.

Her story is a long one, but it begins with that act of hospitality towards Elisha. Was this act merely out of duty, or was she perceptive enough to realise that here was someone different, maybe as good if not better than his predecessor; perhaps there was some aura of holiness about him. Also she noted that he spent a lot of time visiting people – poor people, sick, needy, lonely people – but that pastoral dedication was leaving a tired man, a weary traveller who needed somewhere to rest and rejuvenate before he went on his way. She recognised that even the greatest and most accomplished of men needed to rest occasionally! Even Jesus had to withdraw from the public eye and get some sleep!

But in recognising his need, she didn't respond in the way we might when the minister comes to call, by sitting him down with coffee and nattering his head off! Instead, she left him in peace, gave him space to rest, made him feel at home. In today's parlance, the ideal hostess for the visiting preacher.

Elisha was an influential man. He could have exerted that influence and elevated the woman and her husband to a social position, just by putting a good word in on behalf of the husband, but those things were not on their agenda. It is actually believed that the land and property they had had been her inheritance that had passed to her husband on their marriage – and again, this could have been as a result of her nursing King David in his last days, an honorarium for services given (and may have been the reason for Adonijah's unseemly interest in her). "I belong here," was her reply. "I want for nothing."

That is, except for one thing – that which was more important to Eastern women than any monetary wealth – a child. So that, decided Elisha, would be her reward. Strangely, though, she is reluctant to believe this promise, so doesn't take him seriously, despite all she knows about him. It is, after all, a gift worth far more than anything she might have dreamed of – and hadn't she and her husband been desperate for a family all the years they had been married, and by now they'd probably decided they were too old to try again.

Nevertheless, if reluctantly, they trusted his word and the longed-for son duly arrived. But then tragedy struck, and the child became seriously ill, and finally died. So she leaves him laid in the prophet's room and goes to visit Elisha, whose first question on seeing her is, "Is it well with you – your husband – the child?" He, a prophet, has apparently no idea why she is there, which seems unusual. And she, astonishingly, despite the trauma of the situation, answers, "It is well …" How could she say that? Because she was with Elisha and had faith enough to believe that he could give them yet another miracle. This child had been a gift from God and now he has been taken away – what sort of promise was that, what sort of God would treat a faithful woman so? She had come to Elisha to find out!

It was Elisha's servant, Gehazi, who saw the pace she travelled and realised that something was wrong. When the dam broke and she began to rail at Elisha he feared the worst and tried to stop her, but Elisha, though unaware of the situation, read what he saw aright. She didn't care if it was unseemly to show emotion. She wasn't about to hide her pain from Elisha. She was answering his question in spiritual terms: "It is well with my soul; if it were not I would not be here seeking your help with the physical and emotional pain of losing the son you sought as our reward."

Amidst the tears and anger, hatred and frustration that follow, Elisha despatches Gehazi to check on the child's health, but that isn't good enough for her. She persists until he agrees to return with them. She has faith – but not in Gehazi, not even in God, it seems – only in Elisha.

He capitulates – and finding the child dead, as he'd been told, with no sign of breath when Gehazi laid Elisha's staff on him, he then engages in an exhausting series of resuscitation attempts to which only Gehazi is witness – until the child sneezes – seven times. Seven, the Biblical whole number. But when he is given back to the mother, her reaction is to fall at Elisha's feet rather than before God's altar. Was she giving Elisha more honour than Elisha's God?

She may have been great in the eyes of her neighbours – but what was she in the sight of God? While it appears that following that episode Elisha stayed away from the couple's home, when famine threatened Shunem he did send word to forewarn her so that they were able to move away until it was over.

That, however, raised another problem in which she had to exert herself. By going away from Shunem the rich pair had become poor, for all abandoned land had been requisitioned by the king. In leaving she had forfeited her right to that land, but she was not accepting defeat without a fight. She knew Elisha – the kingmaker – and there were many in high places who were afraid of him. And Elisha knew her too.

The timing was impeccable. When she felt it was right to press her case, she arrived at the King's residence to find Gehazi there already, just happening to tell the king about the time Elisha raised a dead child of a woman who'd been good to him! If the Shunamite woman had anything to qualify her as an Advent Woman, it was that she had had to learn the hard way that God never forgot those who were faithful, even during the times when doubt took over.

This begs a few questions: had she been too besotted with the son to the exclusion of the father? Had her anger at his death been righteous, selfish or malicious? More to the point, what makes her an Advent Woman? Like the daughters of Zelophehad she stood out for her inheritance, even after she had essentially forfeited it. She won her right. She had also not been afraid to challenge Elisha, but was it for the right reason – or because her idol had been proved, in her eyes, to have feet of clay? Or was it, strangely, because when push came to shove she was not afraid to show her emotions, her humanity, despite the coldness of her mask that "All was well"?

Even in the midst of apparent defeat and tragedy, Advent Woman can grasp at the courage of her convictions and believe that all will indeed 'be well'.

Naaman's servant girl was an example of faith in exile. Rather than become encultured by her surroundings she had clung to her faith and served her mistress well, sharing the family's concern at Naaman's leprosy - and through her counsel he was eventually healed, though not without some persuasion and immense challenge to his pride.

One very brave woman resided in Jericho – **Rahab,** the woman with the scarlet rope - not a pious woman, or even a virtuous one, but a prostitute! In a sense she is an enigma. If Eastern names are indicative of character, Rahab was a loser from the start, for her name, a derivative of Ra, the Egyptian god, has been translated 'insolence' or 'fierceness' as well as 'broad' and 'spaciousness.' By birth she was an Amorite, an idolater.

She lived in Jericho, that great walled city - or rather, she lived on the wall, for she occupied one of the mud houses constructed between the two depths of wall, which we might call the equivalent of a 'flying freehold' today, spanning the two at some considerable height. Living on the wall had its drawbacks as all kinds of people, especially strangers to a city, would automatically find themselves on her doorstep asking directions. As far as Rahab would have been concerned, this was excellent for trade.

But like others many would consider disreputable, she had a sense of God that seemed totally out of character. When the men arrived unsuspectingly at the city, they possibly mistook the house for an inn (and perhaps it was and Rahab's business was conducted under-cover). They obviously spent the night there without demeaning themselves, so why did Rahab act as she did?

She actually risked her life by not giving the men's presence away, and instead questioned her motives. Perhaps she didn't know where they were from, but there was something about them that made her trust them (for she, too, could have been in a vulnerable position). There is no doubt that somehow they were led to Rahab's house. They wanted information, and Rahab's reputation and profession would suggest that more than the usual services could be bought: to be paid for information would be easy money, with no scruples attached. For whatever reason they were led to her house, one thing was certain – that they would be less likely to be noticed as strangers than if they had sought a bed at an inn where lots of questions would be asked. Few would be likely to take notice of who came and went at that house on the wall!

Rahab was not, of course, honest - but neither have many others been who have done God's people service. First she pretended they had been clients and left, then she blatantly said she didn't know where they had gone, implying that they hadn't been gone long.

Had she, in fact, an ulterior motive? Some long-standing score to settle with the King of Jericho perhaps? Kings used people like Rahab as pawns in any games they chose to play. What better way to retaliate than take the risk of exposing **him** to his enemies? And she did it so subtly. She didn't deny they had been there, leaving the king's men to assume what they liked. She fabricated an alibi for them so watertight, so plausible as to be unimpeachable. Whatever her motive, she doesn't, on the surface, come out very commendably – yet God used that situation to His advantage.

There has, however, to be more than that. No money changed hands, no gain appeared to be made on her side at all – except for one thing. She was no fool. She knew that the arrival of those spies meant war – the city was about to come under siege, and she was afraid of what might happen to herself and her family. So better be on the winning side!

It was after the king's men had ridden away that she went to the men hidden on the roof, her eyes open to their identity, and made an extraordinary statement of faith - faith born of fear, since Israel's reputation was well-known. She had learnt from their pursuers why they were there. She could have reported them, but that ran risks with her own people. She knew she had to help them, though letting them go could put her own family at risk from the invasion she knew would follow.

But she was shrewd. The reputation of the God of Israel had spread like wildfire and was more fearful than the known factor of the king's wrath. Having no doubts about the power of their God she proposed a bargain - their lives for hers and her family's, with neither needing to disclose the other. It could have been seen as blackmail.

She was also well-informed. This was a woman of the world, well-educated in its ways - and its geography. It is likely that as well as being in her more dubious trade, she could also have been a businesswoman who produced linen from the flax she was drying on the roof and dyeing it scarlet; hence the ready availability of the scarlet cord and a whole lot of subsequent 'trade' terminology. She knew exactly how long it would take their pursuers to return and advised the men accordingly. Hide for three days - a tall order, but it was one set of orders for another as she let them down from her roof: they to obey her, she to remember the scarlet thread that would spare her and her family. It was a situation of mutual trust fraught with danger. It was also an enlightening one, for Rahab had begun an encounter with the Living God while the men had learnt how greatly He was feared.

And the promises were kept - but how did she feel about the carnage, the booty, the bonfire Joshua made of the city, and worst of all, the curse he placed upon it? These were her people. No wonder Rahab had been afraid. What did she think of Joshua and his God as she stood outside the wall watching her beloved city razed to the ground? How she and her family must have wept, and wondered. Her home was not spared the fire, only the slaughter.

Notwithstanding, Rahab and her family made their home with the Israelites thereafter, and she also changed her profession and adopted a settled family life. She subsequently became the mother of Boaz, guaranteeing her a place in the genealogy of Christ, whether or not she was also the wife of Salmon. There is a theory that her husband was actually one of the spies she helped. However, that is a subject of dispute in Rabbinic circles. That apart, and for rather obvious reasons, her faith and courage are also recorded by both the writer to the Hebrews and James.

At a much later period, two other women were brave in different ways - the Persian queens, **Vashti and Esther**, one a queen by right, the other by default. Their story has to be one of the best known next to Ruth.

King Ahaseurus (or Xerxes), who ruled in Susa from 485 to 465 BC, gave a huge banquet for all his male officials. Meanwhile, Vashti, his queen, entertained the women. All went well until, after seven days the king was drunk and wanting a new attraction - and settled on parading his beautiful Queen.

However, Queen Vashti, sober as the day, refused. She was not going to be made an object of entertainment for her husband's drunken friends. She'd been there before, pawed and cat-called. No thank you! As queen she was entitled to some dignity and respect. And who today would disagree?

But it was a brave thing to do in those times and it drove the king to anger and his officials to fear: if the queen could disobey her husband and get away with it, how long would it be before their wives did the same?

So they proposed the sending of a royal order banishing Vashti and at the same time ensuring that it made every man 'master in his own house.' It wouldn't, after all, be difficult to find a new queen, and that would be an example to them all. Quite what Vashti's reaction was we're not told. Perhaps she was relieved!

Consequently, what amounted to a high-powered beauty contest was organised.

So exit Vashti, enter Esther, the adopted daughter of her cousin Mordecai, a descendant of one of the Jews taken into captivity by the Babylonians. She instantly became the favourite of Hegin, the eunuch in charge of the king's harem, though no one knew her origins.

But was Esther being any less exploited by Mordecai than Vashti had been by her husband? At that time there was no way she could have guessed why she was there in that upmarket 'cattle show' which lasted a year. Was it a big adventure, an incredible honour, or a terrifying nightmare?

And what of the outcome when each girl had to go to the king for 'trial' and judgment. At that point she became a concubine in the second harem and saw no more of the king unless she was summoned. One cannot imagine any joy in such a demeaning situation.

We can trace the story of Esther's rise to power in three stages – where she is chosen, challenged and courageous. But we cannot divorce this from the historical background to the events – the powerful reign of King Ahaseurus or Artaxerxes II (as he was also known), who ruled over 127 provinces of the Persian Empire, from India to Ethiopia.

So Esther became the chosen one. Why?

Firstly, without in any way compromising herself, she helped save the king's life. Mordecai had taken up position outside the palace gate so that he could keep one ear on the welfare of his cousin, and another on the welfare of the Jewish nation in Persia. He overheard a plot by two of Ahaseurus' chamberlains to kill their king, and then heard of Haman's plans to eliminate the Jews. Haman was an Amelekite, the Jews' traditional enemy, and old feuds die hard.

Desperate to alleviate the situation, Mordecai challenged Esther to reveal her own Jewish identity and do something, adding that she needn't think she would be immune just because she lived in the palace as queen: if Haman did not kill her someone else would – God would see to it. Mordecai had refused to bow to Haman because he was a Jew and it contravened his religion, so Haman had decided to punish the whole race. In agreeing to Haman's request the king had no idea that his own new wife was among those under threat of death.

Esther got to know through her maids and the king's eunuch, who were detailed to look after her with no questions asked, but it was obvious from the exchanges that they found out her origins, especially when Hathack was sent back with that blunt message, "Who knows. Perhaps you have come to royal dignity for such a time as this."

Poor Esther. She was not easily persuaded, but she knew that if she remained silent she would die, and if she fell foul of the king she would die, but "If I perish, I perish." Three times she hesitated to do something to help her people – until it was pointed out that her own life really was also at stake.

So she took the first open step of faith since her arrival at the palace – and called a fast, for both herself and her servants, as well as for the whole Jewish population. This was something she couldn't handle alone: she needed the prayer support of every one of her people – and she got it.

Of all Biblical women, Esther has to have been the bravest - but she was no fool either. While the Jews fasted Esther plotted, and her first request of the king was not a plea for her people but an invitation to a banquet for himself and Haman.

Did he think it odd, or was this a frequent occurrence in this place? Whatever, they went - and went again - and Haman was cock-a-hoop and off his guard - till he saw Mordecai and in telling his wife, **Zeresh** the idea was hatched by her for a gallows to be made to get rid of Mordecai before the next banquet.

But it didn't work out like that, for the king had a bad night and soothed himself by having the history read to him - and Mordecai's part in saving his life was highlighted. As a result, Haman had the indignity of having to proclaim Mordecai's honour for it. Meanwhile, what Esther lacked initially in courage, she made up for in cunning – as well as self-control. Rather than set about accusing Haman and making demands on the king, she ensured that both were made comfortable in her company, putting them at their ease – and – off-guard – with a meal – and then another. It could have been a dangerous move: Vashti, her predecessor, had been deposed following a banquet. However, it was in this setting that Esther was able successfully to plead for the lives of her people and the purpose of her presence in the palace was consolidated.

Nevertheless, even when Mordecai was elevated and all was revealed, there was still one more request, one more time when she had to risk her life and go to the king, to get him to revoke Haman's destructive letter. But more than that was done as the Jews turned on their enemies and destroyed and plundered them.

And Esther was party to it. Is this where bravery stops and cowardice begins? It leaves a nasty taste to her story, even as she establishes the commemoration of the Feast of Purim - 'The Lot' that almost went against them. The scale of havoc wrought at her request was nothing to be proud of. It would have been sufficient for Haman alone to die and the soldiers called off, with at the most some added punishment for his ten sons, but not wholesale slaughter of the kind planned against the Jews.

Esther is more than a story – she is a valuable stone in the building of the history of God's people. She was brave, but she was used. Yet while the means did not justify the end, it was to a good purpose - the saving of her people. But it changed her from being an innocent beauty into a mature, thinking and fearless woman - of whom, interestingly, we hear nothing more, which makes one wonder ...

Advent Women are brave and courageous when they trust beyond their own strength, but they have to be prepared to take risks, to grow and change if their bravery is to be effective and worthwhile.

SPLENDOUR

Mighty God, King of the universe,
all the wisdom on earth cannot match Yours,
not even the wisdom of Solomon, flawed human being, like
ourselves.

The world You created was perfect
but we have damaged or destroyed so much,
and yet, our God, the wonder is that You still love us, still care for
us.

The Queen of Sheba marvelled at Solomon's wisdom,
at all the splendour of his kingdom.
Not all the wealth she possessed could equal such mystery.

Dear God, may we so value the splendour of Your gifts to us
that the world might open its eyes and see and believe through us.
To Your glory.

15. THE FORERUNNER AND THE PROPHETESS

Luke 1:5-80; 2:36-40

Elizabeth is introduced as a woman with a pedigree - a descendant of Aaron, while her husband, also a priest, was descended from Abijah, another priestly family. They were pillars of the temple in every way, religious and moral. Just one thing was missing from their lives - a child.

She was, of course, in a line which included Hannah, Rachel, Rebekah, Sarah and others - but in time she is far removed from them, living, as she does, in what we now regard as the inter-testamental period.

We might expect that by this time there would have been a more enlightened view on childless women and that Elizabeth did not get hysterical or feel ashamed of her position. Understandably, they had prayed hard in the face of impossibilities, but it seemed to no avail. So maybe it was because they had accepted their situation that God suddenly chose that moment to bless them with answered prayer and begin the fulfilment of His great prophecy through them.

And what a prophecy this was for those two old people! A child who, like Samson, would be subject to the ancient Nazirite rule, full of the Spirit, drawing people to God through his preaching.

Like so many before him Zechariah asked the obvious questions. How? How will I know? Questions which, for a man with knowledge of the scriptures, he shouldn't have been asking. So, having requested a sign he got it - and became dumb - all in the middle of his turn on the temple rota. When she became pregnant, Elizabeth realised that this was indeed the work of God. What she didn't really understand was what Zechariah had been told and why he was unable to speak.

But Elizabeth didn't make a big issue of her pregnancy. Instead, for five months she remained in seclusion because it seemed that one shame had been replaced by another. That seems incredible. Surely answered prayer, especially for one in her position, should have been a cue for calling on others to share her joy and gladness, and more importantly, confirm her status in society.

Then she received a visit from a young cousin, Mary, who, she was to discover, was also expecting a child - and she not yet married!

Nevertheless, there was no room for chastisement. Mary had been told of Elizabeth's pregnancy by the Angel Gabriel and was visiting for that reason - and the moment the two women faced one another Elizabeth's child decided to do a somersault! And suddenly Elizabeth knew. The Spirit came over her and the pieces of the puzzle slotted together, and she was able to identify the relationship between them in spiritual terms, recognising the special nature of Mary's child.

For three months the two of them talked and prayed and planned and sat in awe of God's wonders. Mary left her a month before Elizabeth's baby was due. There was no shame for Elizabeth now. She could attribute her state to the mercy and grace of God and everyone was rejoicing with her.

In those days the family took a leading role in naming children, so naturally they wanted her son to be Zechariah, to which Elizabeth objected. Only when Zechariah had confirmed the name of her choice in writing was he able to speak and tell the whole story to his astonished family.

What would this child of Elizabeth's become? One thing was certain. Elizabeth had to train him towards his Nazirite vow and towards independence, and then let him go into the desert as a recluse when he came to manhood, a hard task for a mother to face, though not unlike the calling of Hannah. But Hannah was blessed with more children, whereas we read nothing more of Elizabeth. It isn't hard to conclude that for Elizabeth the destiny of John would be easier to bear because it would assure her that he would have a place to be when she and Zechariah had gone.

Does that mean that in that one child her work for God and her personal fulfilment were both begun and ended? Elizabeth was given a task which, despite her age, she was given strength to accomplish to perfection.

Advent Women are single-minded. When God fixes the goal nothing is allowed to detract from it - and when their task is completed they let go, leave the result to God and move out of the picture.

Anna's presence in the Gospel is short but sharp. In one sentence we learn her life-story. Her father was Phanuel of the tribe of Asher, one of the lesser tribes, descendants of Zilpah, Leah's maid. She had been married only seven years when her husband died and was presumably childless. Now she was eighty-four, but instead of bewailing her state she had turned to the temple and committed herself to God's service so intensely that she had received the gift of prophecy, which in turn perhaps gave rise to something of a missionary spirit.

Anna never left the temple but she was not a recluse. She had set herself apart for the task of continual daily devotion. As a widow, this was the service she felt she could give. Perhaps long before St. Clare, it was Anna who first inspired other women to set themselves apart for the worship and service of God.

And Anna had been an Advent Woman in waiting for years. Like all true Jews, she looked for the redemption of Israel, and this was the content and purpose of all her words. Now she happened to enter the temple just as Jesus had been taken for circumcision. One look at that baby and, like Simeon before her, she recognised that there, in Simeon's arms, was God's Messiah. In him, she knew, was God's power and purpose to liberate.

And how they both praised and prophesied at this recognition, leaving his parents somewhere between fear and fulfilment, and as she went out praising God for that encounter she assumed a distinctly evangelistic role.

Sadly, the prophecies that day were not all good news. Simeon had spoken of Jesus becoming the salvation of God's people – and not them only, but the Gentile nations of the world as well – the first hint that Jesus wasn't to be the sole possession of the Jewish faith, but of non-Jewish peoples too. He would be there for everyone.

But Mary would suffer deep pain because of him, said Simeon. Did Anna, in her rejoicing, say anything to soften that blow, relieve the situation? Did she urge Mary to enjoy her child while she could for she was destined inevitably lose him one day?

Anna's has been described as 'a waiting faith.' It is an Advent faith.

As an Advent Woman, Anna recognised the point at which the long waiting was over and the promise was beginning to be realised.

TRUTH

Begin the tale –
Tell it straight, as it was,
no frills or quirks or decorating truth –
just as it was.
But how and where, except at the beginning,
a long, long time ago –
somewhere out of town,
a temple in a run-down priestly suburb
where all they had to live on was their faith?
The priest, long-married to his ageing wife
lacked heir –
so little thing today where cutting off
and out is commonplace.
Then it was the Ark revisited –
a message, age, command to faith
and all things in their place.
Now it is a different kind of truth:
flesh and blood – especially blood -
that courses through each century
to tell the truth
and brings an aged worshipper a child.

+++

*Lord, may we, **like Anna**, reflect the mystery of your presence –
the joy you bring us, the peace and blessing, the promise of new life.*

16. JESUS' WOMEN MINISTERS

Luke 4:38-39; 7:11-17; 8:1-3, 43-48; 13:10-17; 21:1-4; 23:55-24:12
Matthew 20:20-28; 27:55-56

Whatever some would have us believe, there were many women among Jesus' disciples. Most, though not all, were numbered among the wives of rich officials or women with their own means, an unusual situation in those days, one might suppose. One reason for helping Jesus was that he had helped them. He also treated them equally. He met their needs and rewarded their faith with no distinction. Though the sins of women may have been different in law to those of men, he had the same compassion for them.

Because the Twelve had no women among them, it is often thought that this showed that Jesus thought them inferior and incapable. It is nowhere stated that the Seventy he sent out were all men. Indeed, it has been suggested recently that the nature and sensitivity of their mission would have necessitated the presence of a woman team member in family and female only situations. [12] Thus they clearly did serve him, in a number of ways. He saw faith in those women and their desire to work with him, though the greatest accolade of all went to the sacrificial commitment of a poor widow who had just two tiny coins to her name, both of which she gave to the temple treasury, which would have been far more well-endowed than she was. Most importantly of all, he welcomed them to listen to him and to share his teaching – and he undoubtedly listened to them.

Jesus also elevated their position in marriage, in which they were generally assumed to be unequal. It was common practice at the time for a man to divorce his wife on any pretext he chose – Jesus saw how loaded this was against the wife and forbade it unless she herself had deliberately committed adultery against her husband, and even then, not if it could be avoided. Thus he set women in a much better 'bargaining position' and gave them higher status as wives than ever before.

The first woman mentioned is identified only by reference to her son-in-law, Simon Peter, the one disciple who is referred to as being married. Jesus had gone to Simon's house from the synagogue and found her with a high fever, quite possibly a very serious one. In one sentence Dr. Luke dismisses both fever and incident. Jesus 'rebuked' it and it went away - and it was as though it had never been. She immediately got up and began to 'serve them' - producing a meal, seeing to their needs - anything at all she could do for Jesus.

Luke also specifically refers to the fact that some women were with him, providing financial and other resources as a result of being healed. Two named are **Joanna** and **Susanna**. Joanna was the wife of Chuza, Herod's superintendent of royal properties and chief steward of his financial affairs, a privileged position that afforded his wife status and a luxurious lifestyle. She must have run a great risk in her association with Jesus, both for herself and for her husband, though it could be that a blind eye was being turned in the hope of gleaning useful information through her.

However, it has been suggested that she had become bored with her lifestyle and that the last straw had come when Salome danced and her greedy grasping mother used the opportunity to get rid of the critical John Baptist. She had become sickened by the immorality and conspiracy at the palace, and in disgust she went out, and that was when she heard Jesus, saw how he had picked up John's ministry and expanded it, and realised that here was a lifestyle which had meaning and purpose. It is even possible that going with Jesus cost Joanna her marriage, publicly at least, since Chuza couldn't afford to align himself with the one man Herod feared more than the Roman Emperor. Yet if that was the case, she can't have gone penniless, even if she was stripped of all other privileges, unless she had independent means of her own he couldn't touch.

So had she been healed? She was certainly an intelligent, thinking, caring woman who did not put herself first, or she would never have put herself at such risk.

Susanna is another so named. She is thought to have been a widow left with independent means, who had been healed by Jesus. Her name means 'a white lily' and gives the impression of a fragile-looking yet immensely tough lady.

Not surprisingly, they were there at his gruesome death when all the disciples had run away. Matthew's Gospel tells us that 'Many women ...' were there, albeit at a distance. Among them was **Salome**, sometimes confused with the mother of James and John, the two sons of Zebedee nick-named in some sources as 'sons of thunder.' She had acquitted herself less favourably when she tried to win preferment for her sons. Of course, she had meant well, Jesus knew - but perhaps he also sensed that this preferment was more the desire of 'the boys' than her own motherly ambition. Consequently, he ignored the questioner and addressed the subjects! Yet she was still there among his loyal servants, but not the Salome who was among Jesus' close women followers.

Advent Women are still human. They don't always say or do the right things!

One notable factor is that while Jesus had to **call** the men to leave what they were doing, those women, healed and therefore given their freedom by Jesus, **went**, voluntarily, of their own free will – and each performed their ministry according to what they had; the wealthy gave them money to buy their food and clothes and other commodities necessary for their itinerant work; some gave hospitality. Rich and poor alike, they were single-minded, and they gave **fearlessly**. And they were all there, right to the end. Their ministry, voluntary as it was, was given out of love and gratitude, and was exercised to the end. There could have been reprisals, from both synagogue and society, but while some of the men hid in fear, their devotion kept them focused and did not waver.

And it was these women who, having followed Jesus from Galilee to Jerusalem and then witnessed his violent death, who stayed around and ministered to him in death - or rather, attempted to, for when they arrived at the tomb they found it empty. He had risen. Their spices weren't needed. They had happened on a momentous event.

Not surprisingly, they were terrified when two angels appeared, but in Luke's account they are calmed down and sent to remind the disciples that what he had foretold had happened.

"Remember how he told you ..." Jesus hadn't just talked to the men and ignored the women. They hadn't merely picked up snippets of knowledge as they waited on the men. Jesus had sat them down and educated them, too, and now the first inkling that that education was to be put to use was being given – and they remembered their lessons well.

Two of those women are named as **Joanna** and another **Mary**, James' mother, and it is likely that other wives or mothers of disciples were also among that number – including more than one Mary for it was a very common name in Jewish families. But what a reception they received! Certainly not respect, nor the benefit of doubt. All Jesus' teaching, all his promises paled into insignificance as those women's message was ridiculed, rejected, trodden underfoot. Stupid women! Gossips! They must have taken to drink – the shock of Jesus' death had been too much. They shouldn't have hung around that cross so long and got involved. Who did they think they were making out that angels had given them a commission to bring such news to **them**? They, the men, had been on the front line, after all. Momentarily, they forgot how fearful they had been, how they had deserted Jesus just when he needed them. It was Peter, the most despicable coward of all, who eventually felt the urge to get up and check it out for himself. So, verified, were they then justified? Sadly, still that act did not seal women's status in the scheme of things.

In his account of the proceedings, Mark even tries to convince his readers that they were too scared even to go to the disciples and tell them of their encounter, which is his way of keeping them in what he perceived to be their place. He does not credit them with either integrity or courage.

Advent Women, with this news of incarnation, will not find an easy passage, but their own convictions will drive them on.

There were other helpers who are not recorded as becoming disciples, yet one cannot imagine that the woman at Nain whose only son was about to be buried did not for ever after bless God for restoring him to her. It caused a lot of fear but it seems unthinkable that this widow was not the foremost of those telling the world what had happened. It had given her new life, taken away shame and poverty. Jesus had met her need that day with her son's life.

Similarly, when a crippled woman came into his line of vision while he was teaching, his immediate reaction was to offer her release from her affliction through the laying-on of hands. In response she began praising God for this miracle - though it did not please the leaders of the synagogue because it had happened while Jesus was involved in teaching on the Sabbath Day.

Where were their priorities? If they were prepared to untie and water their animals on the Sabbath, shouldn't a human being be loosed and freed to revel in the water of life and health? His hearers got the message and rejoiced with her - and they would all go on rejoicing and, led by her, spread the word even farther.

Advent Women will push out those barriers till self and possessions are all one in the service of God.

One woman could be said to have stolen her healing, but that's not how Jesus saw it. He also knew that according to the Law she had contaminated him and made him unclean. He knew, she knew, but one might well ask why anyone else should have known such intimate details of her health, short of the doctors on whom she'd spent her life-savings seeking a cure for persistent haemorrhaging, which must have been so debilitating that it was little wonder she did no more than touch his robe. "He need never know," she thought. "I only need to touch the hem of his robe as he passes near me." She had heard about Jesus and decided to 'give him a try'. He had healed other people – maybe he could heal her. He was her only hope now – but dare she ask him? The answer was undoubtedly that she dare not. To begin with, she was a woman and what she asked would cause embarrassment. Also, it would reveal that she should not be with anyone in the first place – she was ranked as ceremonially unclean according to Levitical law. If she revealed that she would be sent away, her one last chance of healing gone for ever.

She was desperate. All her resources were gone, her dignity, her faith almost. A twelve-year haemorrhage must have left her emaciated. What little knowledge we have of early medical practices leaves little doubt that when the Bible says, 'she suffered many things of many physicians' it literally means just that, and we are told that she grew worse, despite the fact that it was a very common problem in those days, for which the Talmud gave eleven possible cures, a good number of them mere superstition. No wonder she was daring enough to take a big risk.

But was she also naïve? She under-estimated his perception. He knew the instant that healing power had left him.

"Someone touched me!"

"Well, hardly surprising in this crowd," retorted the disciples. "You must be mad trying to single out one person. Come off it!"

Would Jesus have identified the woman if she hadn't felt guilty and confessed? Did he, in fact, turn and look her straight in the eye, compelling her to own up - in front of all those people? How embarrassing.

But how mean if she had kept it to herself and tried to deny what had happened. Healing was for sharing and after twelve years surely there was a great deal to share!

Jesus didn't tell her off for trying to keep her secret. He was a man of compassion. He understood her need. "Go in peace," he told her. "Go and start living, working and being again - your faith has set you free."

And Advent Women need to be free to exercise that faith wherever they are.

But had she stolen that healing at the expense of another – that 12-year-old girl who, by the time Jesus reached her, had died? To outward appearances, yes, and there would be some there very angry at the way she had delayed Jesus getting to the girl. However, the result was an even greater miracle – that of restoring the girl who had died back to life..

But when legend takes over that woman becomes other women - the one who poured ointment on Jesus, for instance, or the one who wiped his face as he struggled towards Calvary, who has become known as Veronica - and she it was who also became a business-woman and provided for the Early Church from her profits.

With Advent Women all things are possible.

HEALING

How could a mother be silenced when a miracle has come into
her life?
Just hours ago her lovely daughter lay sick and then died –
it was the end of hope,
the culling of all her plans,
a darkness overwhelming her.
A tiny promise had come and gone –

Try the healer. He wouldn't reject a child.

He'd set off all right, and then some woman had stopped him
with **her** problem
and that very hour her own child had died –
while the problem had seemed so trivial.

And yet he'd come, purposefully shutting out the mourners,
those who shared her grief –
and that was when it happened:
one touch, one word, and a child bright and well – and hungry.
Such a gift!

But the hardest word of all said *Silence*!

Here was life from death and nobody must know.
Her pent-up feelings broke, her tears flowed –
it was too great a thing to bear.

17. SAINTS AND SINNERS: MARY, MARTHA AND THE MAGDALENE

Luke 7:36-50; 8:1-2; 10:38-42; 24:10-24
John 11:1-14; 20:1-18
Matthew 28:1-16
Mark 16:1-13

Many women ministered to Jesus, but some particularly stand out for their friendship and faith.

Martha and Mary of Bethany are two obvious people, and much has been written about Martha the servant, the drudge, the one left to do all the housework while Mary just lost herself listening to Jesus.

Martha was no saint. She tackled Jesus about the imbalance of their household: "What about telling her to get some work done instead of sitting around all the time like a man or a love-sick teenager, and leaving me to do it all!"

Perhaps that's not quite what she said, but it picks up the tone. She was telling tales: Mary was skiving. She was complaining: "I've got to do all the work myself - feeding you and your friends." She was quantifying the injustice: "It's not fair! I need some help."

Jesus' reply probably didn't help - unless it made her feel ashamed. "You've got your priorities wrong. Being with me and serving God is what matters. We don't need a banquet, you know."

However, despite that rebuke, there is no evidence that Jesus disapproved of what she did do. Extremists see her as the dark side to Mary's light, but that would be to say she was evil, and for that there is no evidence whatsoever. Maybe they were opposites – but not the good/evil type of opposite.

What Martha did do which probably raised a few eyebrows was to complain about Mary and virtually order Jesus to do something in front of everyone in the house; this was no private whisper but a public pronouncement.

What Jesus' reply did was to put her world into perspective. Instead of a small repast she was laying on a feast – one of those trojan hostesses who over-cater and wear themselves out in the process. Martha was too practical - and maybe too generous and lavish in her hospitality for her own good. She was the typical homemaker, bowed down with domestic duties, trying, but in her own strength. She was serving, but in a very human way. Making a hundred sausage rolls is no problem to a Martha; to a Mary the prospect is terrifying!

But what did serving involve? Martha was offering Jesus both her service, and in theory if not in practice, her own meal. For the one who served could only eat when all others had finished, and if there was anything left. That was the essence of being a servant: it involved giving; it was sacrificial. It could be a lifelong commitment. What some people fail to see is that the two sisters had different talents, different gifts, and Martha's were very much the practical ones.

Mary was the contemplative one, but that didn't mean that she was perfect either, or she would have been aware of Martha's struggle without needing to be told, and would have readily chipped in to help where she could. The fact that Jesus captivated her, that she hung on to his every word, demonstrated the imbalance in her life, too. So why did Jesus tell Martha that Mary had 'chosen the better part, which would not be taken away from her'?

Mary was doing one thing that Martha with all her distractions was not doing: listening - listening to Jesus expound the Scriptures, talk about himself, talk about God - and she couldn't get enough of it.

Jesus clearly loved that family, including their brother Lazarus, and saw a great deal of them. In spite of Martha's tantrums, here was a household he felt at home in. It wasn't therefore surprising when he took the news of Lazarus' death so emotionally.

But it is at that event that we see both sisters in a completely different light. When Lazarus fell ill they immediately sent a message to Jesus, and when he eventually arrived it was Martha who rushed out to meet him and this time her chastising was not self-centred but a profound statement of faith – "If you had been here my brother wouldn't have died." But she hadn't finished. "Even now I know that whatever you ask from God, God will give you." What a statement from someone with supposedly no spiritual acumen!

And there follows an unprecedented exchange on the subject of resurrection and life after death which leads to Jesus' explicit statement, "I AM the Resurrection and the Life," and her affirmation, "Yes, you are the Messiah ..."

This was Martha, the busy one, the one burdened with serving, who has faced a personal crisis with the realisation that Jesus had power over death.

Mary meanwhile was still at home. Why? Was it because the possibility that she had anointed him and behaved in an unseemly fashion was true and had afterwards caused her extra embarrassment so that she daren't face him again? Maybe the knowledge of what she had done had added to Lazarus' illness.

Martha knew that the only way to rouse her was to tell her that Jesus had asked for her! And Mary too fell at his feet and before he had a chance to say anything personal, she also declared that he could have saved Lazarus.

But once outside the tomb Martha's faith wavered. No, they couldn't possibly remove the stone. The smell of death would be too great to bear - and she is rebuked, not in words only but in the sight of Lazarus walking clumsily from the tomb.

They were saints, they were sinners. The one thing they had in common was love - their love for Jesus and his for them.

*Advent Women know they are loved, even when they reciprocate in less than conventional ways - for they **are** unconventional.*

The other major woman in Jesus' life, apart from his mother, was **Mary Magdalene**. Mary was one of those who went to the tomb that first Easter Day and found it empty. John tells us that when the others rushed off to do as the angel instructed, she (possibly having missed that encounter) stayed behind, crying her eyes out, her tears blinding her to the reality of Christ's presence.

John has her there alone early in the morning. Finding the stone removed she was beside herself. She had stood beneath that cross and watched him die. She owed him her life and now he was dead and her world was in tatters. She didn't stop to look inside the tomb but frantically ran to tell Peter and John that the body had been stolen. No hint of disbelief there. They immediately set off for the tomb to see what had happened - but while they were inside deliberating over discarded grave clothes, Mary was at the entrance crying. When something eventually did cause her to bend down and look inside she found herself faced, not by Peter and John, who had by then gone home, but angels, who questioned the state she was in.

Still convinced he had been stolen she told them as much, probably not even taking in the celestial nature of her questioners.

And then she turned round and saw a man who, through her tears, she didn't recognise, foolishly assuming him to be the gardener and the perpetrator of Jesus' removal. That is, until he called her name. Then her emotions knew no bounds. Was this a vision, her imagination playing tricks? She wanted to hug him, to touch him, to convince herself that he really was flesh and blood, to pour out her immense depth of love to him. But he wouldn't let her near him. How did she feel then? Was it like having a slap in the face as the only reward for her devotion?

Then, in a split second, she knew he was real - and for her sheer devotion she caught a glimpse of heaven and experienced a miracle large enough to send her flying in all directions with the wonderful news – "I have seen the Lord!"

Did they believe her this time? Peter and John had seen the empty tomb and had already returned and told the others. In the whole of John's Gospel there is no hint that she was not believed.

In Matthew's account the two Marys are alone and experience an earthquake and the sight of the stone actually being rolled away. They witnessed the fear in the guards - but their own fear was allayed when the angel spoke to them, going straight to the point and giving them the message for the disciples. This time they left with fear **and** joy - and were immediately apprehended by Jesus himself.

It makes sense. Someone had to know about the guards and the earthquake and these women turned out to be the most reliable reporters of these things. They had to be to maintain credibility, and there is no hint in Matthew that they were not believed. The disciples followed their instructions and went to Galilee to meet Jesus, even though some weren't so sure when they actually saw him!

Yet in Luke's account the women's report is seen as an 'idle tale' and even Cleopas and his companion found the women's evidence hard to swallow; after all, the disciples had gone to follow up the story 'but they did not see him.'

Even worse, according to Mark, when Mary Magdalene, together with James' mother and Salome, took spices to the tomb and found the stone moved and an angel in residence who tried to calm them and tell them that Jesus was alive, and that they were to take the news to Peter, instead of bursting with the news they said nothing to anyone and ran away in fear.

The earliest narrators stopped there, but others decided that this wasn't right and added the rider which ties in with Luke and John (in particular) that he appeared to Mary - but in Mark's account even the other women didn't believe her - though in fairness, they didn't believe Cleopas and his companion either, and it was as though Jesus had to use a sledge-hammer on the event before someone finally accepted that he really was back!

The shorter Mark cannot – must not - be right. It is unfair not only to women but to those two from the country - as though all were tarred with the brush of excitability and sensationalism or over-worked imagination. Or was he politically motivated? These were uncertain times. Any hint of Jesus being back would result in his followers being arrested for spreading stories. Better play it down. Leave it to the women's excitement but not admit it's true!

Advent Women are not afraid to speak the truth as they see it, nor to share the Good News at every opportunity.

But in Mary's case we need to go back to find the moment her servant-hood began - and Mark, in half a sentence, gives the clue: 'from whom he had cast out seven demons.' Mary, the close companion of Jesus; the most devoted of his women disciples; as near to being a saint as any of them. Yet incredible as it seems, a whole adverse reputation has sprung up for Mary based on just one word - Magdala, her home town and the reputed Red Light district of Palestine, the name of which translates 'tower'. Mix that with the seven demons and the conclusion is too obvious to be true - and Mary goes down unjustly to posterity as a reformed prostitute, a sinner almost beyond redemption.

But wasn't she, rather, the first truly liberated woman? What were those seven demons, or devils? They could have been sins - the seven deadly sins – pride, anger, envy, lust, gluttony, avarice, sloth - for instance. Seven was a Jewish mystical number signifying 'completeness', implying that when the evil spirits dominated Mary her suffering was extremely severe. Afflicted with nervousness, she may have been the victim of violent epilepsy, and when Jesus saw her with her peace of mind and control of will destroyed she must have been a revolting object to look at with her dishevelled hair, staring eyes and sunken cheeks. 'Possession' of this kind did not affect her morals, only her mind. Badness of character is not the equivalent of a deranged mind.

None of the writers tell us the circumstances surrounding Mary's healing – no where or when or why? So what if, instead of the assumption that Mary of Bethany was the one who anointed Jesus at Simon's house, it was actually Mary Magdalene, and either her transformation came at that point, or the anointing was her thank-offering for the healing she had already received? After all, Simon recognised "what kind of woman she was", labelling her "a sinner", adding "If Jesus were really who he claims to be then surely he would know what she's like?" He – and others like him – could so easily have got their labels out of context.

How did this misrepresentation of Mary actually take hold and become perpetuated from pulpits the world over for so long? It goes back to the year 591 when Pope Gregory the Great claimed that she was a prostitute, and the label stuck. It wasn't until 2016 that the Vatican finally redressed that misconception, formally identifying Mary of Magdala as an 'Apostle to the Apostles.'

It is too easy to judge – and misjudge – like the woman who died of sclerosis of the liver and was branded a secret drinker because in 1973 anyone with that complaint couldn't be other than an alcoholic. So there on the death certificate of an honest teetotaller are the words, 'Al-related …' Shamed for death.

Whatever it was that had afflicted and held Mary Magdalene, her encounter with Jesus changed her for ever, and liberated her to the extent that thereafter she wanted nothing but to serve him.

Advent Woman will overcome any adversity when the power of the Spirit of God rather than that of evil is in control.

MARTHA-MARY

My name is Martha-Mary,
a sum of equal parts.
I cannot tear myself in two
imbalancing the scales.
My Martha self is organised,
its servanthood prevails.

If I were wholly Mary
I never could be me
for though I sit at my Lord's feet
and learn to love and trust,
I cannot do it selfishly -
hence action is a must.

So this is not to press one part
against another side –
for Martha-Mary's one whole me,
as seamlessly I'm fused.
If I tried to be divisive
would my Saviour be amused?

No, he doesn't mind my busyness,
my lists and plans and sums,
because he knows behind them
my heart belongs to him.
Thus what I imbibe as Mary
fills Martha to the brim.

18. CHALLENGING WOMEN

Matthew 15:21-28; 27:10,15-19
Mark 12:41-44; 14:3-9;
Luke 7:36-50;
John 4:1-30,39-42; 8:1-11; 12:1-8

Some women offered Jesus a challenge - more so if they were foreign. **The Canaanite (or Syro-Phoenicean) woman** who dogged his steps through Tyre and Sidon while he was trying to escape for some peace and quiet was the classic.

She had heard of his reputation as a healer and she determined that no barriers of race or creed were going to keep her from a share of his gifts.

Not that the request she shouted out to him was a selfish one. Her daughter was possessed, unable to speak for herself, and she desperately wanted to see her healed.

There commenced a ding-dong battle of words in which Jesus tried to rebuff her and each time she came back for more. She was a Gentile - his ministry was to Jews. Was it fair for him to give equal shares to the dogs? Opinion is divided as to whether this is conundrum or insult. The dog was not the pampered family pet we might have in mind. The term was actually a symbol of dishonour, used to describe a 'shameless and audacious' woman in the Greek and as a term of contempt by Jews.

The woman was audacious all right, and she was ready for him. Rather than feel the insult she gave a rejoinder: "Ah, but the dogs eat the crumbs ..."

He was impressed - by her faith, maybe by her humour in the face of his insults, and in her persistence in asking for something she wasn't entitled to according to the Law, though it was unlikely that would have stopped Jesus.

Why, then, was he so hard on her? Playing her up, testing her faith, knowing full well the anguish that lay behind her desperate request. Or perhaps it was something to do with his disciples' attitude. They would rather he had treated her like a dog and sent her away with nothing. They were only human. But he was divine. Surely, whatever they thought, he couldn't remain silent, then quiz and humiliate the woman so mercilessly. Had he, for once, turned his back on someone in desperate need? Was this to be a case of unanswered prayer? Or was he testing her faith to the limits? They could have been forgiven for thinking the worst of him at that moment, of believing they were seeing a cruel side of Jesus they hadn't seen before, or expected to see.

It was her faith in his ability to heal that won her the day, but something else, too. She had recognised, or at least acknowledged, who he was before many of his own people had tumbled to it. She didn't leave that exchange empty-handed. Her daughter was healed.

Advent Women are not only persistent and resilient; they are perceptive and open to persuasion of the truth, as this woman was when face to face with Jesus.

One foreign woman might have served him better than he knew had she been given the opportunity. In just one verse Matthew tells us that the Roman **wife of Pontius Pilate** (sometimes referred to as Claudia) tried to warn him to leave Jesus alone. Through a disturbing dream - a nightmare even - she had recognised his innocence.

Perhaps the question Pilate put to the priests, asking what evil Jesus had done took account of his wife's words, but it is clear that the voices of the priests and their cohorts were louder.

Advent Women are perceptive, but frequently ignored - yet they are not forgotten.

That little bit of humanity slotted into this most vicious of narratives has been picked up by writers and commentators for two millennia, and while maybe stretching the point to its extreme, Mel Gibson in *The Passion of Christ* has produced a really sensitive account of her 'bit part' in the drama.

The women who challenge Jesus are seldom named. One such woman did so, not by words, but by her action, which to the onlookers was hardly commendable. In Luke she is presented as **a woman of questionable morals**. Jesus was dining at the home of Simon the Leper (an identifier that clearly takes account of the fact that he is one who has been cured by Jesus). This woman gate-crashed the party, carrying a jar of expensive perfume which she cracked open over Jesus' head.

The protest that follows was enormous - not so much because she shouldn't have been there but because of what was considered waste. How much could have been done for poor people with the price of that ointment!

Jesus disagreed. He knew his fate and accepted her action as an anointing: "She has done what she could." That act would be her memorial.

The greatest significance is that it seems to have been that act that triggered Judas' decision to betray Jesus to the priests. He couldn't see the sense of it.

As an Advent Woman, she had been attuned to her inner promptings, and so could do no less than give to Jesus the most costly thing she possessed.

In John's Gospel the woman is presented as Mary of Bethany and the setting is not at Simon's house, but at her own home, since it would have been surprising for Mary to have been the kind of woman to unbraid her hair in a mixed gathering and make such an apparent spectacle of herself, especially as she had had enough opportunity for intimate access to Jesus in her own home - unless this was an act intended to be kept away from her sister, but again, it doesn't ring true. Mary she might have been, but not that one. As has already been suggested, this could even have been Mary Magdalene.

An obvious question would be, are all these accounts relating to the same incident? In Mark she breaks the ointment over him and he declares the act will be remembered for posterity. In Luke, she comes as a sinner, loose hair, loose morals, and pours out the offering as a sacrifice - an atoning sacrifice. She doesn't stop short at anointing him but washes his feet with her tears and dries them with her long hair. He accepts the love and forgives her sins - and commends her faith!

But Mary, far removed from these, in John's account, is the quiet sister who just wants to be close to Jesus.

One of Jesus' biggest challenges came as he made his way through Samaria, an area alien to Jews because of its association with what had been the old Israel that had apostasised and been destroyed.

Nevertheless, the old familiar landmarks remained, and one was Jacob's well at Sychar, so reaching it Jesus sat down to rest in the noon heat while the disciples went shopping for food.

A Samaritan woman approached with her water jar. "Give me a drink," he said when he saw her. No 'please' - at least, none recorded.

The scene is reminiscent of the time long before when Rebekah was approached by Abraham's servant with the same request. Then there were no questions but the offer to water the servant's camels. Jesus had no camels - but there were plenty of questions.

To begin with, she was astonished that he should even speak to her. "You, a Jew, asking me, a Samaritan, for a drink? It's unheard of!"

Jesus is challenged, not so much by the woman but by history and the rampant racism that had grown out of it.

Obviously she had no idea who he was, and he capitalised on that. "If you knew the gift of God - and if you knew who I am, you'd be asking me for **Living** water, and receiving it."

"But you haven't even got a bucket and the well is deep so where does such water come from? Are you trying to claim that you are greater than our ancestor Jacob who gave us this well - yes, and even drank from it himself, all those years ago?"

Jesus perceives that she knows her history - and that she is one who has maintained belief in the One God. He deflects her question.

"Yes, but all those who drink this water will be thirsty again - but drink the water I'm offering and you'll never be thirsty again, because it will become a spring of water flowing into eternal life."

She sees the potential of not having to face traipsing to the well at the height of the day to avoid meeting the other women, and pleads with him to give her that eternal water.

That's when Jesus turns the tables and really gets the upper hand. "Go and call your husband and come back." A reasonable order, since protocol would have suggested that they shouldn't have been so long together, unaccompanied.

"I haven't a husband," she admits, perhaps shamefacedly - or a little uncomfortably.

"You're right there," he answers, quick as a flash. "Actually, you've had five and the man you're living with now isn't your husband. You're very honest about it."

Taken aback, no doubt, but nevertheless recovering her composure very quickly, she eyes him quizzically. "So, you're a prophet. Now our ancestors worshipped on this mountain, but you Jews say that people ought to worship in Jerusalem."

So, she knows her history **and** her theology and her eagerness for argument is unabated.

114

But is Jesus wearying of it by now? He presses his point. "Woman, believe me, the time is coming when you'll worship the Father neither here on this mountain nor in Jerusalem. The difference now is that you don't know what you worship, but we do - for salvation does come from the Jews."

"However, the hour has now come when all true worshippers will worship the Father in Spirit and in truth, for He is seeking out those who worship Him in this way. God Himself is Spirit and those who worship Him must do so in spirit **and** in truth."

Has she kept pace with this profound teaching? "I do know that the Messiah, the One called Christ, is coming, and when he does he will explain everything to us."

Is Jesus, who has emphasised the dividing line of worship between Judea and Samaria, surprised to find that even a Samaritan with an unorthodox background still cherishes the Messianic hope? For if one woman does, there must be others ...

So he makes his own confession. "I am He, I who am talking to you right now. I'm the One."

Before she can make any rejoinder the disciples return, shocked to find him alone with a woman - perhaps even more taken aback when she abandons her water jar and rushes off to tell the neighbours she's been avoiding that she's met this incredible man who knows all about her and who claims to be the long-awaited Messiah.

That Samaritan woman's life was changed completely, in more ways than one. Head knowledge became heart knowledge as he plumbed the recesses of her life and she unashamedly gave her testimony to all who knew her - maybe not least those who had known and disapproved - and she was a splendid witness, for when they saw and heard her the others wanted to hear and believe for themselves. And this was a foreign country.

Quite possibly, that woman was one of his toughest challenges short of the actual crucifixion. That one encounter must have significantly paved the way for the Gentile revolution that was to follow the Jewish leaders' rejection of Jesus. He predicted it would happen. Through the testimony of one woman he had begun to see it come about.

But what about **the adulterous woman**? Even the translators are challenged by her. Did this incident happen or not?

Given the nature of it, there has to be too much authenticity to question it. The Scribes and Pharisees were constantly trying to trap Jesus by inciting him to judge hypothetical situations or questioning his compassionate actions. How much better to have a real life case to bait him with?

So here is this woman, silent before her accusers, being argued over as though she were no more than an item on paper.

How did she feel? How afraid was she? She wasn't denying she'd done wrong. She knew it - temptation can be strong but doesn't always contemplate being found out.

The conversation is about her, over her, never **to** her. She watches Jesus write in the sand and if she can read the words it must either amaze her or terrify her even more. At last he stands up. This has to be the moment of truth.

"Let the one who isn't a sinner throw the first stone," he declares. She closes her eyes, waits, prays that death will come soon, if it must, then becomes aware of the ominous silence. She opens her eyes to find Jesus again writing on the sand - writing quotations from the Law or the Psalms perhaps.

Then she realises that a miracle is happening. In the profound silence, one by one they are dropping their stones and creeping away. Jesus stands up and looks around, and pretends surprise to find only the woman in front of him.

"Where've they gone?" he asks. "Hasn't anyone condemned you?"

"No one, sir." They are the only words she speaks and her tone will tell him all he needs to know about her state of heart and mind. "Then I don't either," he says to her. "Go home now." But then he adds, quietly and firmly, "but don't do anything like that again."

The narrative is told too quietly, for it belies the nature of the challenge the woman's presence poses and takes no thought of her own reaction, which must have been one of stunned disbelief. Could she possibly be the only woman ever to commit adultery and not die for it?'

She was a test case for the Scribes and Pharisees to use against him, and once more he had confounded them. But she, already *in extremis*, had been cruelly used.

Advent Women challenge the system. They question the accepted norms. They work for understanding, for change, for a better life. Yet they are not afraid to admit when they do get things wrong and welcome the opportunity for a second chance.

There is one more woman, already referred to but worth mentioning again, one who said not a word but challenged the system by her action. She has been described as the reckless woman. We are told that she was a widow, **a poor widow**. We are not told her age, but somehow imagine her as old and bent, struggling up the temple steps in rags, her face wrinkled and drawn, her hands bony and blistered from years of hard work. Had she been younger her condition may have been different, as she may have been able to earn a few pence and not be so dependent on charity.

This old woman loved God. She demonstrated this by her giving. Jesus could not have known her personally, yet he recognised the manner of her giving: sacrificial. She was a poor widow and he could tell how much she had given in comparison with the rich people. He did not criticise those who paid into the temple treasury for doing that, or the system of collection that was in place. He viewed it in perspective - and it was their motives he criticised, not the system. She gave everything, holding nothing back. The fact that the sum total of her giving was less than a farthing, which in more modern terms would be less than one sixteenth of an old penny, meant nothing to Jesus. He judged gift and giver together and that made all the difference. The widow was giving all she had to God and when all material wealth had gone, there would be the practical service at the end of it - for material things can create a barrier between the servant and God. Giving to be real giving must be sacrificial, and giving which is real giving has a certain recklessness in it. And this widow was reckless. She didn't stop to think where her next meal was coming from; she threw in everything, perhaps two precious coins she had just been given because she had not eaten that day.

She had no idea that the Son of God himself was watching what she did. Her mind was intent on the worship of the Father and her desire to give Him everything she had.

Advent Women are reckless, but they will never want for the abundance of God's blessing in their lives.

WATER

He asked her to share, that was all,
to share a bucket full of water,
a cup to quench his thirst.
He didn't care about hygienic niceties –
death would come soon enough.
What mattered was this moment -
his thirst in the noon-day heat,
her unrealised need for Spirit food.
Death has many connotations.

How little did she know except her history,
the broad span of sectarian division,
the attitudes, the image of a God
worshipped in opposing views,
in temple or on mountain-top,
despising one another. All that
and a life of legal immorality
come to nothing, leaving her outcast.
He knew. He came with Life.

He had no bucket, no outward affluence,
she had no inner lasting view.
"My water lives," he said,
"but you will come again all your tomorrows
drawing water in the noon-day sun.
I will free you now and give you so much more
and you will know the secrets of eternity
and never have to fear reproach again –
I know your history, but I can heal."

He knows us all, and still the water freely flows
and he is healing now.

19. EARLY CHURCH WOMEN

Acts 5:1-11; 9:36-42; 12:1-17; 16:11-24; 17:22-34; 18:1-21; Romans 16:3-5a

The first woman named in the accounts of the Early Church was not an Advent Woman. There had been many blatantly evil women in the Old Testament, women who were seducers, pagans, enemies of God - women who led their menfolk (and others) astray. These are not Advent Women either, but nevertheless there was a distinct difference: **Sapphira** could have become an Advent Woman, one with power and wisdom, if only she had not colluded with her husband in his act of deceit.

In those days the Christians held everything 'in common'. Everything they owned or received was shared, not by force but quite voluntarily, which meant that had Ananias sold the field and he and his wife agreed to take money to the disciples and say, "This is X% of the sale of our field" nothing more would have been said. Nor would it if, having been made aware of his intentions, Sapphira had dissuaded him. But she didn't.

Instead she went along with it - to the death. The shock of exposure killed Ananias; the dual shock of exposure and Ananias' death killed Sapphira. The Church shuddered and saw it as a judgment. Coming so soon in the infant Church's life it was not a welcome occurrence but seen as the action of a vindictive God.

But this account does tell us one thing. Women were not automatically punished for what they did not do. Sapphira was treated separately and allowed to speak for herself. She may well still have collapsed at the news of her husband's death, but she could have told the truth when she realised they knew. She was regarded as an individual thinker.

In contrast to Sapphira, who was condemned by her own words, **Tabitha** was raised to saintliness by her deeds, so that when she died there was a huge mourning for her.

Tabitha, or Dorcas, 'the gazelle', was a disciple who lived in Joppa, or Jaffa as it was later known, a busy seaport with a history that goes back beyond Israel's entry into Canaan. She may or may not have had a husband - he isn't mentioned (again, a departure from Judaism). She had become a disciple in the coastal church founded by Philip, which served as a centre both of evangelism and well-organised and far-reaching social service, to which Dorcas made a very large contribution, using her gifts to the benefit of others. But she was not simply a do-gooder seeking to emulate Christ in all the ways open to her, creditable though that might have been. She was, first and foremost, a **believer**, one who had surrendered her life to Christ and then said, "Lord, use me in whatever way you can," – and the Lord had done just that.

She must also have been well enough off to afford to make and give away so many clothes to poor people, especially widows, and she was also held in such high esteem that the disciples at Joppa sent for Peter to come to them.

Why? To try and placate the mourners? To give her the funeral she deserved? Surely not to raise her to life! Yet the real impact of her story centres, not on the fact that she lived but that she died – and **then** lived again.

Peter arrived to find mayhem on her doorstep - all the widows holding up what she had made for their children. The message was clear: they wanted Dorcas back – not so much for Dorcas' benefit, but their own! Perhaps she had done too much for them.

That was when he ejected the lot and with a Christ-like compassion knelt by her bed and prayed - and then told her to get up!

There is no other record of what passed between them but those women had had no doubt about her death: they had laid out her body, ready for the funeral. Instead, the sound of rejoicing must have been far greater than that of wailing.

Why was Dorcas raised? Was it simply to comfort the many mourners, to show God's compassion towards them, and in order that she might resume her good work? Or was there some deeper reason? When Jesus healed someone his words were often, "Your faith has made you well." In this instance, whose faith? – Dorcas' in her lifetime, Peter's in believing that he could do this through prayer – or was it that of her fellow believers who, hearing that Peter was in neighbouring Lydda, sent an SOS – "Please hurry and come to us"? Did they, when they sent that message, seek comfort – or a miracle?

Of course it added to the Church, but there is no question that Tabitha's own self-giving had already done much to proclaim the Gospel to those in need.

*Dorcas **was** an Advent Woman.*

The early years were times of great unrest and persecution for the young Church but some constants remained - like the women who continued to form the nucleus of the cause and meet practical needs as they had in Jesus' time.

One of these was another **Mary**, this one the mother of John Mark, reputedly the compiler of the first Gospel. It was at her house that the last supper had taken place prior to Jesus' arrest, so it was not surprising that the disciples continued to meet there. Thus it was to Mary's house that Peter went on his unexpected release from prison. He knew that from the moment of his arrest they would have been praying for him, so who else should witness the answer? She is clearly remembered most for her hospitality, which could have put her at risk with the authorities. They were times of intense persecution. To openly hold prayer meetings in her home laid Mary bare to maximum risk of arrest, imprisonment, torture, even death.

But what about **Rhoda**, the maid who recognised Peter at the gate and was so eager to tell the news that she left him outside? Her name, which meant 'rose' was a common slave name in the Roman world and suggests that she was Greek, possibly from Cyprus. Quite in what capacity she was in Mary's house is unclear, but from the little we read about her it would suggest she was more akin to an 'upstairs maid' than a scullery slave. She is obviously not afraid to burst into a room without due ceremony in the middle of a prayer meeting. The irony is that she has just not answered the door to the answer to their prayers. Perhaps her first reaction was fear, or maybe, hearing the knocking, she was playing for time and wanted to give her mistress and the others time to hear and to compose themselves in case it was any of Herod's men come to arrest them or spy on them. Then when she heard Peter's voice, knowing him to be the very person for whom they had been praying because news of his arrest was on everyone's tongue, she was so overcome that instead of opening the door to him she rushed off in an unseemly fashion to tell everyone the news.

But what happened? They couldn't believe her! However, she refused to be fazed by their attitude or browbeaten by the incredulous reactions of those who had just risen from their knees on Peter's behalf.

"It's Peter!" she exclaimed, wild with joy.

"Don't be ridiculous, girl. It can't possibly be Peter. He's in prison. Haven't we just been praying for him? You're imagining things. You're mad." And the word they used meant literally 'insane.'

"No I'm not," was her response. "It **is** Peter. See for yourselves." And as the knocking persisted they had to go and answer the door, regardless of who it might be.

Typically, once more a woman had good news to share and wasn't believed! But is it equally typical that when our prayers are answered we can't believe it's happened?

Advent Woman would be like Rhoda - the first to believe - but would she leave the answer to her prayers standing at the gate?

During their travels Paul and Silas were apprehended in Philippi by **a slave** who possessed 'a spirit of divination.' As soon as she saw them she drew attention to them and declared that they were 'proclaiming a way of salvation.' Now she could have been harnessed, or Paul could have taken the lead and capitalised on what she was saying - but no! Instead he got annoyed and commanded the Spirit out of her, in the Name of Jesus.

Sadly, we don't hear what happened to this slave girl. She had been set free from possession, but not from ownership, so very likely in real terms there was no salvation for her, only greater slavery. If she managed to escape during the ensuing furore, should the record not have told us?

How often Advent Women are those who are used and then discarded! When their message has been delivered or their healing accomplished, they are no longer of value: the 'show' has moved on to the next attraction.

It was to the Jews that Paul's mission had first been headed, despite a few wider encounters. When he reached Corinth he found a Jewish couple who were to play a significant part in his ministry - Aquila and his wife **Priscilla**. They had been in Italy until the emperor Claudius had expelled all Jews from Rome.

Like Paul, Aquila was a tentmaker so it was inevitable that they would establish an affinity and even set up business together. That meant that they worked at the trade in the week, but on the Sabbath Paul was in the synagogue arguing with both Jews and Greeks - until he couldn't take the opposition any more and declared that from then on he would be preaching only to Gentiles. When he eventually left the area altogether Priscilla and her husband (now referred to with Priscilla as the first-named) accompanied him as far as Ephesus. The two, it seemed, were inseparable in ministry as in marriage, though there is a body of opinion that suggests she was the stronger, more forceful and even more 'upmarket' than her husband.

In Ephesus Priscilla and Aquila found their own ministry. They came across Apollos, a Jew on fire for Jesus, but not yet baptised into the early Church. Priscilla and Aquila filled in the gaps of his knowledge and then sent references with him to Achaia, where he, too, performed a valuable ministry.

Writing to the Romans, Paul asks a special message for 'Prisca' as he now calls her, and Aquila to be passed on to them. They had, he tells the Romans, "risked their necks for my life" and that was no small matter, but from this we gather that a branch of the Church met in their house, independently, for in those days there were no church buildings, only groups of believers who often relied on Paul to link them together, and sometimes didn't see eye to eye.

📖 📖 📖 📖 📖

GAZELLE

Her name was Dorcas – the gazelle,
light of heart, of feet, of touch,
nimble fingers working seams
creating miracles from scraps,
discards of the rich
who paid their tailors handsomely
while she worked hard for love,
not only of her neighbour,
but her Lord.

How she was loved for all she gave.
Those widows thought the time would never come
when needle, thread and life would be laid down.
She was immortal in their eyes.
But came the day when sickness took its toll
and she, worn down by giving,
had no strength to overcome,
so lost the fight –
and how they mourned.

Weeping all the while they tended her,
with loving final rites as best they knew.

"If only there was one who could have come
and laid their hands before our friend had died!"
Was there some vain, unlikely thought
that even now some miracle might pass?
This was God's work for she His loyal soul
had given all for others –
was there hope?

They sent for an apostle, half-hoping he would come,
though why, in truth, they did not know.
Meanwhile they still maintained
the mayhem of their mourning night and day –
till Peter came and sent them all away.
He looked with great compassion at their need,
and then surveyed the worn-out soul laid there.
He knelt beside her, gently took her hand
and prayed his hardest, willing God to hear.

Then, "Tabitha."
He whispered her sacred given name
at which her eyes awoke
and shone into his face, so graciously.

Where had she been in that deep sleep of death,
what had she seen beyond her worldly toil?
Had he snatched her away from Paradise
and flung her back into the world of strife?
Her work was not yet done, she realised,
but as he led her out to face her friends
perhaps he remonstrated in her sight
that they had asked too much before,
taken her for granted, taken all.

Now she was spared to train another one
to learn her trade and take the Lord's work on.
No one should feel alone, however much
they stay committed to the task.
God asks we give Him all
but no more than He gives us strength to do.

When next the loved gazelle danced on her way
fresh hands were there to take her mission on,
and she could reconnect with Paradise,
assured the work begun would carry on.

20. WOMEN IN THE WORLD

Acts 17:22-34; 16:11-15

Paul didn't seem to get on very well in Athens. Scholarly opinion is divided as to whether he did the Gospel any service at all there, because he was using Greek rhetoric to explain a subject that was alien to the Greek culture of which it was a part.

Yet the point at which he was leaving brought a number of people to him confessing faith. They included a woman named **Damaris**, one of only two people named. Damaris is referred to in only one line, but because of the setting something can be known of her, and scholars have been able to piece together some idea of who she was from the various records of the time.

The Greeks, like the Hebrews, set some store by the meanings of names. Damaris means 'heifer'. The first thing to consider is that she was at the Areopagus at all. This was the place of the philosophers, but the Greeks, like the Jews, had places where few or no women went, and this was one of them; certainly not for any woman from a good family or social standing, for it was the place where murder trials took place and cases of civil disobedience were dealt with. It is therefore thought that she may have been one of the *hetairai* or companions of Ancient Greece, a group of women who were educated similarly to the Japanese geishas: specifically tutored to give entertainment to men! The kind old-fashioned moralists would call 'fallen women'.

However, others have assumed her to be the wife of Dionysius the Areopagite mentioned in the account, but there is no evidence for this, especially as Dionysius, a member of the court, would be unlikely to have taken his wife there. Again, the text refers to 'a woman called Damaris' whereas, had she been his wife, the record would have said so. That leaves the possibility that she had some other form of relationship with Dionysius, perhaps an extramarital one, and to the writer of Acts this would have been noteworthy. Nevertheless, the fact that she is named affords her some level of distinction; even more so the fact that both of them became believers.

Some manuscripts omit her name altogether, which could imply that since no respectable woman would have been in the market place, Damaris' conversion was one from following a profligate existence to a more positive and Godly way of life. In fact, any connection with Dionysius falls down when Eusebius, in his church history, informs us that Dionysius eventually became Bishop of Athens.

As it is, we hear no more about her, but the very mention of her name suggests both a dynamic conversion and the fact that she was no transitory believer and that the Church was well-acquainted with her.

Sometimes a very brief reference indicates a big story, and the first of these was the lady in Philippi described by some as the first convert. But **Lydia** was already a 'God-fearer'. She worshipped God as opposed to any pagan deities, and with a Christian rather than Jewish understanding of Him. Clearly, the distinction lies, not in the level of belief, but in initiation. She had not previously been baptised, but as soon as she heard Paul preach she made that commitment. She was a very positive person. Hers was no emotional flight of fancy, but a sound, reasoned decision.

And then she went further. Like the Shunammite of old her service was to include hospitality, and she put them on a spot if they refused ...

"If you have judged me faithful ..."

How could they refuse? Here was a woman, a rich city businesswoman, who gathered with other women to pray on the Sabbath and who was unafraid to go public on her praying. If they declined they would be casting doubt on her faith. They had to set their Jewish scruples about single women aside if they were to fulfil their purpose among the Gentile converts. And besides, they could do with a decent base to stay at ...

Possibly there was a two-fold purpose in this. They needed hospitality; she needed encouragement, needed to know she was getting it right, needed to learn how to maximise her opportunities as she worked.

And maybe she even knew - and they undoubtedly knew - that that infant church needed people like her to give it money and respectability. That was what happened in early Methodism. When the philanthropists moved in they not only funded the churches but gave them respectability. Yet they, like Lydia, were people with strong faith and zealous commitment.

*Advent Women may be women in the world, but once committed to the Gospel, they are not **of** the world.*

COMMERCE

Father God, You call us out of the commerce of life,
You set us apart, teach us,
answer our questions, and say
This is your place,
the work I want you to do.

Sometimes, God, that work is easy,
at others it is very hard and unrewarding
and we wonder why and where and how.

And at times we see the reward,
the fruit of our labours spread before our eyes,
and we marvel that You used us in a miracle.

Lord God, when we doubt, grant us hope,
when we weaken, make us strong,
when we lose sight of our goal,
show Yourself to us afresh and work a miracle in us.

21. WOMEN BEYOND THE BORDERS

Romans 16:1-16, 21-23;
1 Corinthians 16:15-19;
Philippians 4:2-3,18;
Colossians 4:15,17;
Philemon 2
2 Timothy 1:3-7; 4:19,21b;
Titus 2:1-5

Writing in his letters, Paul often makes reference to particular women, some of whom we know little about, yet from the context in which he writes we may infer much, one thing being a greater equality than either Judaism or subsequent practice allowed.

Writing to the Romans, Paul begins by greeting 'the saints'! And the first thing that stands out is that **Phoebe**, a woman, is described as a minister – and one whom Paul is anxious to support.

But what kind of ministry? Pastoral, diaconal, presbyteral? Paul wasn't short of making distinctions and didn't use words unadvisedly, and nor does he use the term of anyone else. Also, there seems to be a hierarchy and she is top of the list.

Phoebe is ministering in the church of Cenchreae. She appears to have been of Greek origin since she is named after the Greek Moon Goddess, Artemis, commonly known as Phoebe. It is thought that this Phoebe may well have been the very first deaconess of the early church, though it is also conveniently assumed that her ministry was to women only, despite the exceptionally high regard she merits from Paul. He had also appointed her as bearer of his letter, and is asking them to welcome her on to their staff.

We learn also that Phoebe is a benefactor, which implies that she is a woman of means who has given money as well as time and talents to the Church and to those in the Church, Paul included.

Advent Women are open and generous but would not expect this to take the place of active service in the Church.

Further down the line are other women, most one half of a couple. These are the hospitable ones. And then there is yet another **Mary** "who has worked very hard among you." Which Mary is this? One

128

of the Gospel Marys now part of the general scattering of the church, or a different one altogether? As Mary is a Jewish name it is supposed that this was her baptismal name. She is most often referred to as Mary of Rome. The reference suggests that she has been a very hard worker for the Gospel, perhaps as a member of one of the groups of women evangelists, something akin to that of today's Salvation Army.

The real significance of this Mary is that Paul mentions her at all. That indicates one of those tireless workers who labour with little thanks and spend themselves out, and the smallest word of love or encouragement, even a simple personal greeting like this, speaks volumes and means so very much. This Mary mattered, not for anything grand but simply for being there and getting on with the job.

Advent Women are prepared to work hard and go anywhere God calls them.

And **Junia**, variously referred to as Junias or even Julia. It appears that this lady was a relation of Paul's, possibly wife of Andronicus, though others have described her as either wife or sister to Philologus. He refers to them being in prison with him, and that is possible, as initially he was under house-arrest but with freedom to entertain whoever he chose. He also makes the surprising remark that they are not only leading Christians, but that they had already become Christians before Paul himself had encountered Christ on the road to Damascus - perhaps keeping well away from him to avoid persecution! She is thought to have been a member of the Imperial Court, and therefore one of the Christians actually within Caesar's household.

Paul also mentions **Persis** who has 'worked hard in the Lord.' Her name, 'taken by storm', has been linked to Persia but there is no evidence for this. It could, however, be deduced that she took the world by storm in her approach to the preaching of the Gospel.

Then there are **Tryphena and Tryphosa**, assumed to be two sisters from a noble Roman family, possibly deaconesses, and their contribution must have been outstanding for Paul to take such notice of them. Archeological evidence found in Christian cemeteries substantiates their place, not only in the church, but in Caesar's household.

The last chapter of Paul's letter to Rome is far more than a mere list of acknowledgments. It is an exceptionally valuable historical document containing twenty-six named Christians as well as many, such as Rufus' mother, who are not personally named. Was she, in fact, the wife of Simon of Cyrene, who carried Jesus' cross? It is more than likely. And though translations vary, it is also more than likely that Rufus' mother, whom he describes as 'mother to me,' was like a 'second mum' to Paul, and as such highly regarded by him. For the fiercely independent, often arrogant Paul to write such words says a great deal for and about her.

In Philippi we have **Euodia and Syntyche**, hard workers for the Gospel along with Clement, yet perpetually at loggerheads! It is possible that they were converted along with Lydia and therefore participants in those riverside early prayer meetings Paul encountered. So why were they at variance with one another? Personality clash perhaps? Whatever it was, they were disturbing the peace of the Church.

Sadly, this is a situation too often repeated in our churches today. An elderly minister once told me of two sisters in his congregation, very committed to the Church, very active, but perpetually feuding with each other. At every Communion service they would be kneeling at opposite ends of the rail and all efforts to reconcile them failed miserably – and he felt his responsibility deeply.

Advent Women may be outspoken, but they must also be reconcilers.

The letter to the Ephesians contains mention of no women, and this may be because it is not even clear that Paul wrote that letter, but rather that it was someone writing in his name and assuming the misogynistic attitude mainly associated with him.

Two of the most well-known of Paul's female friends, from Lystra, are **Lois and Eunice**, grandmother and mother respectively to Timothy, his disciple and co-worker whom he was training for leadership. Lois, the only person referred to as a grandmother in the Bible, is described as a woman of 'sincere faith', a faith which he clearly sees that Eunice has inherited.

Lois, a Greek name, means 'agreeable or desirable', similar to the Hebrew Naamah, and this seems to reflect her character. She was a Jewess, obviously by that time a widow, or she would not have been living with her daughter. Since there is no reason to suppose that she had married outside the orthodox Jewish faith she was, therefore, a devout Jew. All that seems to have changed when Paul arrived in Lystra, having been drummed out of Iconium, and began preaching and healing. Through this Lois was persuaded that Jesus was indeed her promised Messiah so she became a believer. Her conversion probably did not change her a great deal, except to make her take a new look at some of the legal trappings of Judaism. She was already a devout woman, and, we learn from Paul, her grandson's spiritual instructor.

Eunice, 'conquering well', was her daughter, perhaps named more in hope of some 'good and happy victory' than prophecy. Or was it? Eunice seems to have battled all right, with tradition, her family, and probably also with her in-laws, for she had committed the 'unforgivable sin' of marrying a pagan. It was an easy thing to do, situated as they were in a Greek province. Lystra was in Galatia, in Asia Minor (modern day Turkey). He was probably a soldier who had come along and swept the young Jewess off her feet, and maybe at that time love definitely had the edge over faith.

Hardly compatible with all the wonderful things Paul and most of the biographers seem to be saying about her, but do they paint too rosy a picture of Timothy's upbringing, for when Eunice married a gentile, she automatically excommunicated herself from the orthodox Jewish community? This may well have been the reason her son was never circumcised, though she gave him a significant name, 'one who fears God.' By the time Paul came into their lives it is assumed she was a widow, and this made her, like her mother and son, open to the Gospel, from which time they all became committed workers for the Christian cause. The inference in Paul's letter is that they provided a Christian home for Eunice's son which made him the person he became in God's (and Paul's) service.

Some of those mentioned in his letters to Timothy had left him, others were described as 'apostates from the truth.' However, **Claudia** and others had stayed with him and sent their greetings. It is thought that Claudia was the wife of Prudens and that Linus, who eventually became Bishop of Rome, also mentioned, was their son. Many legends abound round Claudia's name, but there is no proof that they relate to the same person. One has the sense that Paul greatly valued the help and support of Christian women and held them in higher esteem than we might at some times suppose.

When he wrote to Titus in Crete it was in an attempt to sort out problems within the Church there. Many of the older women were irreverent, slanderous and undisciplined in their habits. He wants them to about turn and set an example for others to follow, not one they must not. This is Paul's less favourable side. Women, it seems, were always intended to be examples, and of course, those he found most exemplary were so, without needing to make a special effort.

Advent Women do not need to be told to set this or that example. Their whole lives will reflect Christ - yet they will retain their own identities and be true to themselves even as they are true to him.

One thing becoming abundantly clear to more recent Biblical researchers is that in the early church women were on a par with men – even to the point of becoming bishops – but all that changed in 312 when Constantine won the Battle of Milvian Bridge under a flag bearing the Christian *labarum*, the monogram in which the two Greek letters X and P (the first two of Christ) intersect, forming what is referred to as the XHIPHO (Chirho) symbol. Assured that this had given him the victory he not only became a Christian himself but converted the whole of his empire. However, being a military man, he deemed the church a male only territory, and in consequence, women were no longer able to minister on equal terms. And that situation remains within the Church of Rome today.

CHERISHED

What gentleness, what love streams from the heart of God,
spreading out to those who seek
and filling them with love and care.
How valued then they feel themselves to be,
how greatly cherished, even when they fail.
And then how loyal!
These are the quiet souls who lay their lives and burdens at His
feet.
who die with Him, and live again,
who share His pain and suffering
without complaint.
These He will embrace
and open wide the gates into His heart.
For these He set the stone of His approval,
they are His own, so marked
with His own scars
that they can never turn aside
to follow other ways.

And with such love and gentleness they seek the lost,
comfort sad and lonely in His Name,
and speak His peace
to troubled hearts.
They are His hands, His lips, His voice,
His listening ear,
His running feet
that go the extra mile
for Him.

22. MARY THE MOTHER OF JESUS: ULTIMATE ADVENT WOMAN

Luke 1:26-38; 2:1-7, 21-40, 52; 11:27-28; 23:55-56
Matthew 1:18-25; 2:1-12,16-23; 12:46-50; 13:54-58;
27:55-56
Mark 3:31-35; Mark 6:1-6; 15:40-41,47
John 2:1-12; 19:25b-27
Acts 1:14-15

Lord, help us be like Mary,
committed, loving, brave.
She gave You her obedience
to help the world to save.
She suffered shame and hardship,
fulfilling her set role -
the Mother of our Saviour,
the One Who makes us whole.[13]

The fourth Sunday in Advent - **Mary's Day**, and Advent would not be complete without the Ultimate Advent Woman.

But this woman is a contradiction in terms, a confusion of whole woman and absolute obedience. She can never be a woman in her own right for she will always be The Mother - *Theotokos*, the Mother of God, *Christotokos*, the Mother of Our Lord, the Mother of Christ Jesus, the supreme example of motherhood, the universal Mother, regardless of which Christian denomination one belongs to.

What would Mary, the over-awed teenager whose name meant 'bitterness', engaged to the carpenter of Nazareth, have thought if anyone had told her that one day she would be called the Queen of Heaven? Regardless of the prophecies surrounding his birth, Jesus himself refuted any blessing to her when an unnamed woman called out "Blessed is the womb that bore you ..."

Much has been written about her - and **to** her. Perhaps too much. Too much that ennobles her beyond reason, elevates her to unthinkable realms, makes her an object, reduces her femininity and literally turns her into an idol. How can we find the Advent Woman behind all these trappings and trimmings? Only by returning to the Gospel record and putting her back into her authentic context.

And fortunately, Doctor Luke, with an eye for the human element of any situation, has done just that. He introduces her as a young woman with an older relation who has just been the subject of a miracle - and now she herself appears to have been chosen for some special task - or has she?

Sometimes, while sharing the horror of an unmarried, uninitiated teenager, we fail to see the significance of the marriage to which she is already committed. We know two things about Joseph. He was a carpenter, and he was a descendant of King David, and nothing else about him or her really mattered except that second factor.

The prophets had always foretold that the Messiah would come from the House of David - not an easy option to fulfil considering the way the tribe of Judah had been exiled and scattered and persecuted over the centuries.

Now logic would suggest that a woman of the house of David would be appropriate, but Judaism being a patriarchal religion, that wouldn't do: even if the woman was of the Davidic line, as Mary herself was, he had to descend through the male line.

One now enters the Blakean realms of depicting God, His eyes roving the world contemplating every eligible descendant of David in order to identify the most appropriate - and that would be the one about to marry a girl innocent and unsullied by the world, for she was the one who would bear the greater part while the husband simply had to be persuaded that it was all right for him to give this unexpected child his name!

In other words, though the more 'romantic' would disagree, Mary was chosen less for herself than for the name of the man she was to marry. Had he borne the ancestry of any other clan she would never have reached the first page of the history books, let alone the Bible.

Hardly a promising beginning for the Ultimate Advent Woman! But perhaps that is exactly why Mary now receives the excessive veneration some give to her - not to attempt to outdo her Son but to emphasise the fact that she and not Joseph was the key player in God's great Incarnational Drama. Indeed, the evangelical wing of the Church now tends to ignore Joseph altogether.

While earthing Mary in reality, the Biblical narrators actually do her the greatest injustice of all time, and maybe it was no wonder that some in the Early Church felt she was being neglected.

We know nothing more of her background beyond her relationship with Elizabeth, a descendant of Aaron, and it is that alone that saves her from being completely eclipsed by the claims of the House of David. Everything else written about her parentage and the claims of her own immaculate conception are legendary and not founded on either known fact or Scripture.

As far as Mary was concerned, she was a normal young woman of a hugely moral disposition looking forward to marriage when suddenly she was confronted by this strange angelic visitor towering over her, and her world fell apart.

After all, girls like her did not become pregnant before they were married. It was not done in respectable families like hers! The shock must have been earth-shattering. The squeaky clean Gospel account makes her too submissive, too cool for comfort.

Probably what really made the bizarre visit believable were his words about Elizabeth. The whole family would have shared Elizabeth's grief at her barrenness. Had she not been made aware of that miracle Mary would never have dared to go and visit her cousin during her own pregnancy. It would have been insensitive.

Mary was only able to accept God's will because she was a devoted believer. Even though she managed to ask a few questions, only if she had been a waverer would she have backed off. If she herself **was** chosen it was for that alone.

At that juncture we need to switch to Matthew's account, where the record is balanced by an angelic visit to Joseph while he slept, no doubt unhappily thinking how he had been betrayed by the girl he planned to marry. That, of course, made sure the marriage took place before the world became aware of her condition - even though it would appear to those with inquisitive minds that all had not quite been done in order.

Joseph, too, had to give in to God, and it probably hurt his pride more than that of Mary to do so. Yet he, too, was obedient. Thus the potential for the family unit was created.

Shortly afterwards Mary discreetly pays her visit to Elizabeth - somewhere in a Judean hillside town which for some odd reason isn't named. Up to that point we have two human mothers, both of whom have conceived out of due time - but suddenly the evidence begins to dawn on both how special their children are. Not only is Elizabeth delighted to welcome Mary, but so is her unborn son.

An interesting question here is whether Elizabeth was expecting Mary's visit and whether she was aware of her condition beforehand. The question has exercised novelists to various degrees but we aren't told - only that the sound of Mary's voice provoked an unexpected response from her own child.

Mary's recorded reactions are the words of what we know as the Magnificat. Whether she really composed such a song at this moment in her life we don't know. It could be a summary of many thoughts and feelings, or the interpolation of the Gospel writer. It does, however, provide the only Biblical justification for the reverence in which she is held.

By the time Mary returned home, her condition probably raised no eyebrows, and Elizabeth was about to be the centre of the family focus.

If we think of Mary in terms of facing hurdles, that was the first. The second looms at almost the time she herself is due to give birth - an event by now prepared for at home with the midwife booked and her family in attendance. That is, until the Emperor decided to hold a census, and not having benefit of computer or even a postal service adequate for the task, there was only one way to tackle it - send every man back to his birthplace, and too bad if his wife wasn't really in any condition to travel.

Luke dismisses the birth rather abruptly, giving no hint of the terrible dilemma the couple faced when the inns were full and there was nowhere to stay. Joseph had probably intended to stay with relatives but babies don't wait for the most convenient moments - not even when they are the Son of God!

Poor Mary! An ignominious way for any woman to give birth, though not unknown even in the 21st century Western world. That night more than any other she must have grown up very quickly.

And this was no sterile white environment for a new baby, but a cold, smelly stable with no warm bedclothes and no hope of peaceful sleep - especially when the visitors started to arrive.

Children love the Nativity story while adults are often far too content to leave Jesus in the manger and forget he ever grew to manhood and to the ministry for which God had prepared him. So great things are made of visiting shepherds, and the chronology goes out of the window to accommodate the Eastern mystics.

But for Mary these events must have added to her confusion. The shepherds reported how they had heard about Jesus and we are told, not that Mary made any response, but that she quietly remembered what she had been told and thought about them endlessly, wondering what it all meant.

The next hurdle arose only eight days after all this when she was probably still weak from her ordeal - but the Law decreed that her baby had to be circumcised and named. The record in Luke is a little oblique but Matthew tells us that it was Joseph who gave Jesus his name as commanded both by protocol and the angel.

Later still, they took him to Jerusalem for the Purification - or thanksgiving for birth and what would be the equivalent of 'churching' in some denominations.

Here they find themselves in what should have been a routine ceremony faced by Simeon and Anna, a devout Jew and a prophetess respectively. And this old man took Mary's child in his arms and prophesied about Jesus' role in the destiny of Israel, and then told her that "a sword will pierce your own soul, too." Anna, on the other hand, praised God for his coming.

What was Mary to think? Did she, even then, have a sense of foreboding about her child's future? Given the circumstances of his birth there had to be something.

And somewhere in all this was the visitation of those strange men from the East who hailed him as a king and gave him extravagant gifts of the kind this modest family were unlikely ever to have seen before - but they were gifts to be discreetly managed in order to ensure a secure future for him - and how they had needed that money when, instead of staying in Bethlehem, they had been forced to escape for their lives and settle in Egypt - another hurdle. Did Mary realise how many mothers were robbed of their children so that hers could live? If she did, what a dreadful burden to live with.

So eventually they settled in Nazareth, from where they made their annual visits to Jerusalem, and where Jesus was able to grow up in a secure environment.

Mary's next hurdle arose on one of those temple visits, when Jesus was twelve, and of an age for his bar-mitzvah, which marked his graduation to manhood. What did she think when he went missing? Certainly not, "I've lost God's Son - what will He do to me?" His identity was the last thing on her mind. This was her son and he was lost, and she was frantic, so it was hardly surprising that when she found him in the temple she became really angry at his nonchalant greeting, and big as he was, called him to order - and the conversation is as natural as any might be ...

"Your father and I have been searching ..."

It is not Joseph, the adoptive father, who chastises Jesus but his mother - yet she refers to Joseph as his father - the public persona.

He meanwhile throws a poisoned dart into the ring: "Didn't you know I must be in my Father's house?" And while the rest of the party and the priests didn't understand what he meant, Mary knew, and even though her son obediently returned home, she went on thinking and storing up all those titbits of information in her heart and mind, wondering what the outcome would be, knowing even then that she had lost him.

And then, in one sentence, the remainder of their time together is summarised by the fact that Jesus became wise and well liked by God and humanity alike. The tone is almost dismissive.

By the time Mary is back in the record Joseph has dropped out of the picture, presumed dead because it is assumed he was much older than Mary when they married, as very often happened when marriages were arranged between families. Only by inference do we learn that the family must have grown apace during those early years, dispelling all the theories of 'perpetual virginity' that have crept in around her. Nor is there anything to tell us what kind of marriage it was or whether Jesus' position in the family ever caused friction between them, as well it might. To the world Jesus is 'the carpenter's son' or 'the carpenter' which implies that as eldest he took over the family business till he began his itinerant ministry.

It was then that Mary began to face the hardest hurdle of all - rejection, something most mothers dread and many have to suffer - but should Mary have had to be one of those when her son was the Son of God?

And he did it in the cruellest way. Of course, the worst thing that can happen to a son, particularly a prominent one, is to have his family follow him about, but when this happened to Jesus he responded with what amounted to disowning them – "Who are my mother and brothers?" And rejected them in favour of his disciples and others who were living according to God's will! Hardly the way to influence them to believe in him.

Was that really fair on the woman who had risked ridicule and rejection in order to give birth to him? That sword promised by Simeon had already begun to strike home.

At some point when Jesus had begun to realise his call to ministry he was baptised by John and then began to gather disciples, as every itinerant rabbi did. Even so, he seems not to have left home altogether, as John tells us that he and his disciples were with his mother at a wedding at Cana.

From the account in John[14] it is clear that Mary has more than begun to see where God is leading her eldest son, so when the wine runs out she appeals to him for help. His response? "What concern is that to either of us?" They aren't part of the family, just guests. He doesn't even address her as his mother - just "Woman" in a tone of reproof. But he adds, "My hour hasn't come!"

Mary will have none of it. "Do as he tells you," she persists in addressing the servants. What could he do? She had cornered him till he had no option but to help - and we perceive that there was some strong affinity between the bridegroom's family and Mary. Rightly or wrongly, Mary knew he was capable of saving the day - but was turning harmless water into gallons of best wine the right use of God-given powers? The quantity alone suggests a kind of back-hander: "You wanted wine - well now you've got it - oceans of it!"

It saved the wedding so could be said to have done some good for the bridegroom and his family, but did it present Jesus in the way God intended or give a false impression that here was another miracle-worker, a magician who can turn water into wine - a desirable party guest?

In her zeal did Mary, like Eve, persuade her son to do what was not acceptable in God's sight?

"My hour hasn't come," he had said. Worse still, we read that his disciples believed in him then because of that miracle rather than anything he had said to them, or what he was in himself.

The account ends with all of them leaving for Capernaum, his mother and family included. But according to the other Gospels, at some stage Jesus retreated to the desert alone and when he returned he was a different man and nothing was ever the same again. Was the fact that he had not yet made that retreat the explanation for his words, "My hour hasn't come. It's too soon. I'm not ready"? It would disturb the chronology of other events, but it is feasible. Perhaps the rebuke given to Mary later indicated that on no more occasions was he going to allow her to distract or mislead him.

Much later, when he has been away and returns to Nazareth with his disciples and speaks in the synagogue, utter amazement is expressed that this 'son of Mary and the carpenter' should possess such talent. Why, they knew Mary and her large family too well - James, Joses, Judas, Simon - and an unspecified number of sisters. Who was he to speak like that? So they took umbrage and were offended - and they completely sapped his power. He spoke of prophets having no honour in their own families. He'd been in Cana when his mother persuaded him to perform a miracle, but they'd heard of it, surely. Was it that some unseen hand was staying his and preventing him from listening too much to his mother, or her family?

For most of his ministry Mary is kept in the background, and it is his friends who take on the roles of supporters, later as mourners, and finally as news-givers. Frequently he hurts her and ignores her, and John was probably very conscious of this and felt for her, since it appears that he had lost his own mother.

Was that why he included that little episode by the cross, when Jesus looked down, saw the women, and especially his mother, part of the crowd yet one alone, except for that attentive disciple? At the height of his suffering Jesus seems suddenly to become aware of her need. He is leaving her. Who will care for her now, especially in her grief? Answer: John.

"Woman, take care of this lad as though he were your son."

"Son, take care of this woman as you would a mother."

And so the two were brought together and Mary's future role was assured. We aren't told what her family thought of this arrangement, but perhaps they knew their mother better than anyone and recognised her unspoken need of someone to care for and worry over - a role none of them could fulfil any more.

As she was there at the beginning of his ministry, so Mary was there at the end - but not according to Matthew who singles out Mary Magdalene and another Mary, plus Salome, but not his mother among 'other women.' Luke refers only to 'the women who had come with him from Galilee' and Mark likewise. Only John makes reference to her presence at the crucifixion.

Similarly, she is not mentioned as being present at the resurrection by any of the Gospels. In fact, but for John's record she might as well have faded out of history there and then, which begs many ongoing questions. Luke, however, records that she was present with the disciples in the upper room, praying along with all the others - praying for what? Simply in response to Jesus' command to pray and wait. What we find from this is that not only his mother but his whole family were there with the disciples - a family that, to all intents and purposes, had not believed in his ministry during his lifetime but were united at his death. We certainly know that James, his brother, became bishop in Jerusalem and was martyred some time between 62 and 63 AD.

From that moment on we are working with assumptions - that Mary was with them at Pentecost and received the Spirit along with the disciples, that she was an active member of the Jerusalem church - but nowhere are we told anything further about her.

So, to return to where we began, why the veneration, the titles, the raising of her status? The most likely reason is to address a perceived injustice that God, having used her, had now discarded her to become no more than a distant shadow in the Jesus story.

The Ultimate Advent Woman cannot be kept out of the story!

FAMILY

Who are my brothers - my sisters – my mother?

Harsh words from one whose Name is Love.
Ask "Who is your Father?" and the answer comes as swift as light
for He is Holy.

"My brothers must be Spirit-led,
the ones who do my Father's will,
embrace Him, trust Him, love Him till all time is fled.

My Mother?
She who knows the suffering love
of blindly following God's way.
One day hailed a Queen by those
who need someone more real to pray
their little worries to: I'll understand.

Meanwhile, today, I'm telling you
the way into the Father's heart
is wide, wide open, way past earthly kin,
to all who will believe, repent, come in
and join with me to play their part
in God's ongoing saving task.

Who then, are brothers, sisters, mothers all?
You ask, not short of querying my call
or telling me I have no love because
I ask the question.
Why not?
The invitation is for everyone.

My family is the world -
and one day other ones will come
and mark and claim the territory for their own
and I'll be there:
the world will be **my** Parish, too."

Epilogue

WE <u>ARE</u> WORTHY

Lord, it was to women that you revealed the resurrection glory –
and no one would believe them.
Still we have situations where no one believes us
even when we know you've called,
instructed us, set us on our way.

Lord, open the eyes of the world and tell them we are worthy.
For why, if we are nothing, have you gifted us
and made us love and care and be for others, and for you?
Why, if we are nothing, have we identity to those who need us?
Why, when we know that your commission to those few became
our affirmation,
are we not everywhere proclaimed as one?

Lord, we are ourselves each one, and know **you** care,
as you cared enough to heal and recognise the worth
of many in your day; you listened to their hearts
and took their burdens, questions, had compassion, fed their
intellects.

And through the years you called your saints
in harsher, darker days than these:
they gained respect through your discipling.

So why, Lord, can your Church today
in all its many groups and forms,
not welcome us on equal terms,
assess our human not our gender worth
and use the gifts we readily give back
much more appropriately
than simply making tea?

NOTES

1. Ecclesiastes 12:12b, NRSV
2. *Women of the Old Testament: 20 Psychological Portraits*
3. See *Daughters of Eve: Characterisation, Authenticity and Poetic Licence in Bible-based Narrative Poetry,* No.4 in Christianity and Literature Series [Feather Books, Shrewsbury, 2001]
4. 2 Kings 4
5. *All the Women of the Bible,* pp.3-4
6. *Paradise Lost* Book IX
7. *Looking God in the Eye: Encountering God in Genesis,* p.9
8. *Women of the Old Testament: Studies in Womanhood* [Service and Paton, London, 1898] p.8
9. cited in *Looking God in the Eye,* p.47
10. See C. S., Lewis: *Till We Have Faces: A Myth Retold,* a novel based on the myth of Cupid and Psyche. [Collins Fount 1956, Still in print]
11. *Women of the Old Testament,* p.viii
12. Helen Bond and Joan Taylor: *Jesus' Female Disciples: The New Evidence,* Channel 4 Television
13. From an unpublished Hymn, *Gift of Christmas* by the Author, set to the Tune: *Tyrolese* [Tyrolean Carol Melody, arr. Martin Shaw, 1875-1958]
14. 1 John 2:1-12

BIBLIOGRAPHY

There are many books written about Biblical Women, of which I have read or referred to a considerable number. Inevitably, some are dated and out of print, though they have been useful in determining both the context and changing perceptions of the people studied. Some of the reference books, such as the valuable series by Herbert Lockyer, have been reissued many times and are still in print. Others may be found in second-hand shops, book fairs, on-line and especially at the Alsager Book Sales run on behalf of Englesea Brook Museum of Primitive Methodism. Most of the books included in this list are of more recent origin, useful for more in-depth study or as more detailed accounts than this book contains.

BANKS, Lynne Reid *Sarah and After: The Matriarchs* – Bodley Head, London, 1975 [Novelistic account]

BARKER, William P. – *Everyone in the Bible* – Oliphants, London, 1966, 1967

BAUCHMAN, Richard – *Gospel Women* – T. & T. Clark, London, 2002

BIBLE SOCIETY, – *Into the Light* – Contemporary English Version of the Bible. The Bible Society, 1997

BRIGGS, Richard S. – *Fairer Sex* – Grove Books Limited, Cambridge, 2015

BROWN, Raymond et al – *Mary in the New Testament* - Geoffrey Chapman, London, 1978

DEEN, Edith - *All the Women of the Bible* – Harper Bros., US 1955; Independent Press, London edn.

DENNIS, Trevor –
Sarah Laughed: Women's Voices in the Old Testament. SPCK, London 1994
Looking God in the Eye: Encountering God in Genesis – SPCK © 1998

DUFF, Mildred – *Esther, the Queen* – O & M, Leicester, 1974 [short study]

GAVENTA, Beverley Roberts – *Mary – Glimpses of the Mother of Jesus* – T. & T. Clark, Edinburgh, 1999

GRASSI, Joseph – *Hidden Heroes: The Female Disciples of Jesus* – Marshall, Morgan & Scott, London, 1989

HEBBLETHWAITE, Margaret – *Six New Gospels – New Testament Women Tell Their Stories* – Geoffrey Chapman, London, 1994, 1995 [Part fiction]

LANG, Judith – *Ministers of Grace: Women in the Early Church* – St. Paul Publications, Slough, 1989 [especially chapters 1 and 2]

LAUCHBACH, Frank – *Did Mary Tell Jesus Her Secret?* – Marshall, Morgan & Scott, London, 1970 [Includes study of the Virgin Birth]

LEVENSON, Jon D. – *Esther* – Old Testament Library, SCM Press, London, 1997 [commentary]

LOCKYER, Herbert - *The Women of the Bible* – Zondervan Publishing House, Grand Rapids, 1967. Pickering & Inglis edition. [Still in print]

LOFTS, Norah - *Women of the Old Testament: 20 Psychological Portraits*, Religious Book Club, London 1950

LOUTH, Andrew – *Mary and the Mystery of the Incarnation* – An Essay on the Mother of God in the Theology of Karl Barth. SLG Press, Oxford, 1976

MOLONEY, Francis J. – *Mary - Woman and Mother* – St. Paul's Publications, Slough, 1988

PEARSON, Helen Brach – *Do What You Have the Power to Do* – Upper Room Books, Nashville, 1992

RICCI, Carla – *Mary Magdalene and Many Others* – Burns & Oates, Tunbridge Wells, 1994

RIVERS, Francine – *A Lineage of Grace* – [Tamar, Rahab, Ruth, Bathsheba, Mary] Tyndale House, Illinois, 2002

STORKEY, Elaine – *Mary's Story, Mary's Song* – [focus on the Magnificat] Collins Fount, London, 1993

TIDBALL, Dianne – *Esther – The True First Lady* – Christian Focus, Rossshire, 2001

TRIBLE, Phyllis – *Texts of Terror: Literary-Feminist Readings of Biblical Narratives* – SCM Press, London, 1984, 2002

VON BALTHAZAR, Hans-Urs – *Mary for Today* – St. Paul's Publications, Slough, 1987, 1989

WRIGHT, David F. – *Chosen by God: Mary in Evangelical Perspective* – Marshall Pickering, London, 1989 [Includes study on the Virgin Birth]

Acknowledgments

My thanks to Mark Lilley for permission to use his photograph of the Wirksworth *Knit and Natter Nativity,* to Ashbourne Methodist Church for permission to include my photograph of their Nativity Tableau, and to Jayne Archer for permission to use her father's drawings.

Also to Moorleys Print and Publishing for affording me the opportunity of finally putting this book into print.

As ever, my thanks are due to my friend, mentor, and on this occasion severest critic, **Rev. Dr. Derek Webster**, whose initial assessment sent me back to the drawing-board resulting, I hope, in making this a better book!

The Author

Patricia Batstone spent her formative years in a Warwickshire village near Leamington Spa, where she was accredited as a Methodist Local Preacher in 1964. In the early 1970s she moved with her husband and children to the Hull area which gave her an opportunity to further her education, resulting in degrees in Theology and Religious Education and Literature. In 1987 she was awarded a Ph.D. in Religious Education and Literature by the University of Exeter. Previous publications include a trilogy of prayer books – *Prayers for Worship* [1997], *More Prayers for Worship* [2009] and *For Many Occasions* [2018], plus *The Bound Lamb and Other Reflections* [2013] and *Reflections on a Journey* [2017] – all published by Moorleys of Ilkeston, plus *In Debt to C. S. Lewis* [Cottage Books, 1999] and *The Mystery of Methodism in Honiton* [Honiton Methodist Church/Teamprint, 2005]. She currently lives with her husband, Geoffrey, in the Derbyshire Dales. They have two sons, one a Methodist minister, one a further education teacher, and two student grandsons.